RECONSTRUCTING
THE PAST
to Create a Remarkable Future

By Tony Fahkry

Foreword

I love hunting for the next book that shakes my world and awakens me to new ideas and fresh perspectives. It doesn't happen enough, but I'm pleased to report that this book does exactly that. There are many books that come into my orbit. Many are good but occasionally one is excellent – this is one such book.

All too often we get stuck in a groove of past habits or history – bolted to the floor with our ideas, with no forward movement. Tony's book not only reminds us that we can free ourselves at any time we wish but offers 1,000's of ways to make that leap into freedom. For that reason alone, this book is priceless.

Tony teaches a simple and compelling way for anyone who wants to grow out of their past. They can do just that – if they apply the ideas he reveals, grow and keep growing.

Some of these ideas are: cultivating success is not a straight line, reclaiming your life, and advice on not to wait for the perfect time is always a timeless reminder. There's more in the book, of course. Much more.

I enjoyed the book owing to its uplifting effort to communicate how we are not limited to the conditions of our past. It's a key to unlock your mind so you can reach for the stars.

Read it and apply the lessons. And keep it next to your bed to read and reread again. This is the kind of book you will want to dip into again and again, for inspiration and information. It's food for your soul.

Dr. Joe Vitale

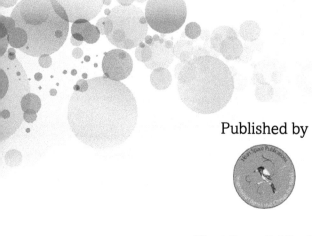

Published by

Heart Space Publications
PO Box 1085 Daylesford Victoria 3460 Australia
Tel +61 450260348
www.heartspacebooks.com pat@heartspacebooks.com

Published in Melbourne in 2016.

ISBN: 978-0-9924338-7-1

To learn more about Tony Fahkry's work, go to:
www.tonyfahkry.com

Introduction

Part 1: Let Go of The Past

Part 2: Create a Remarkable Future

Introduction

I want you to recognise that while you are a product of your past, it does not define who you are now or will be in the future.

The person you are today results from every thought, emotion and belief formed over the years. Whilst your past shapes your current reality, it should not define who you intend to become in the years ahead. This idea is a catalyst, or defining point that allows you to, with intent, design your future outcome.

Every decision ever made has led you to this point in time with a level of awareness clear to you. So who you were in your teenage years is not the same person you are today.

While I state the obvious, many people unwittingly recall their past mistakes and regrets, while overshadowing the present moment. To remain attentive and mindful to the past allows us to create our life's circumstances, imbued with enthusiasm and curiosity.

Mindfulness has become a popular movement nowadays, owing to the growing number of programs, courses and books offering to teach the principles espoused in Eastern traditions. The practice invites you to bring your thoughts to the forefront of your mind, then allow them to subdue you by acting on impulsive thoughts.

Mindfulness is a call to become aware and awaken to your inner world. You cultivate an inner awareness and presence of your predominant thoughts and feelings, thereby allowing you to notice the inner shifts, rather than be consumed by runaway thoughts and the ensuing emotions.

My interest in the self-help movement became clear to me through the number of people I have worked with over the years. It became obvious to my clients, that as they managed their incessant thoughts with a compassionate heart. Those same thoughts no longer dominated their lives and they were at peace in both their personal and professional lives. More importantly, their health improved since they learned to turn down the volume on the endless thoughts which threatened their inner wellbeing.

So what does this mean to you? Consider the last enraged thought you had when an inconsiderate driver cut you off while driving to work. Reflect on the thoughts and emotions which flooded your body and mind in those split seconds.

To react to the outside world has become a common event that road rage is now a term found in Webster's Dictionary. We **react** rather than allow fleeting experiences to pass through us. I am not suggesting we become enlightened monks overnight, yet we can disallow external events to shape and define us, by remaining attentive to our inner world.

Comparable to a ship sailing through stormy waters, chances are it will make its way to safer waters if it does not resist the current or force its way.

Your mind is much the same. Each thought and accompanying emotion has the power to derail your homeostasis if left unchecked – that is your inner state of equilibrium. Many of us do not find the time to engage in self-examination, yet wonder why life goes astray when we fail to connect with our deepest self.

In the same way, if you hear a strange noise from your car's engine, you should have it checked out by your mechanic. Whilst I'm not implying we check in with a mental health professional, we have the wherewithal to become our own psychologist by noticing the ebb and flow of our thoughts and emotions before they wreak havoc in our lives.

As we attend to this, we connect with our inner world, while learning the language of the heart, which communicates to us through silent whispers.

Reconstructing The Past to Create a Remarkable Future will allow you to connect with your deepest self. To reconstruct the past is a call to heal and make peace with unwelcomed events which you continue to carry into the present moment – thus stealing away from your highest potential.

The following passage by Katherine Ponder is testament that forgiveness, compassion and an open heart are the doorway to bringing peace to a troubled past, *"When you hold resentment toward another, you are bound to that person or condition by an emotional link that is stronger than steel. Forgiveness is the only way to dissolve that link and get free."*

This book is divided into two parts.

Part I is titled, **Let Go of The Past**. The chapters contained within Part I will help you to make peace with the past while creating a remarkable future, devoid of the associated baggage.

Louis B. Smedes' quote reminds us, *"Forgiving does not erase the bitter past. A healed memory is not a deleted memory. Instead, forgiving what we cannot forget creates a new way to remember. We change the memory of our past into a hope for our future."*

I invite you to create a new way to remember the past, without the ensuing emotions, thereby leading to a powerful and compelling future.

Part II of the book is titled, **Create a Remarkable Future**. The chapters contained within this section will guide you toward forming a powerful script for the future, by honouring the wisdom that lives within you.

There are no exercises to perform throughout the book. There are no lesson plans, no questionnaires or quizzes to undertake. I have structured the book so that the knowledge and material will offer you adequate resources to awaken your potential. This potential has always been stirring within, yet until now was not called upon.

This is about to change.

I welcome you to *Reconstructing The Past to Create a Remarkable Future* and trust by the close of this book, you will have formed the mental and emotional wherewithal to bring empowering changes to your life, which you have long hoped.

I wish you much success, health and happiness.
TONY FAHKRY

PART 1
LET GO OF THE PAST

CHAPTER 1

Accept Yourself As You Are

"I now see how owning our story and loving ourselves through that process is the bravest thing that we will ever do." — Brene Brown

It was the British psychologist Robert Holden who said, *"No amount of self-improvement can make up for any lack of self-acceptance."* Your subconscious mind interprets every internal conversation as either empowering or disempowering. It therefore manifests to form the relevant circumstances and events according to the mental stimuli it receives. I opened this chapter with a quote from Brené Brown who wrote a wonderfully insightful book called *The Gifts of Imperfection*. Her quote reminds us that **owning our story** and loving ourselves is the greatest gift we can bestow upon ourselves. I have often overheard both sexes refer to others as *damaged goods* or *having baggage*. The inference, tied to intimate relationships denotes the likelihood of a person to bring their emotional trauma (as baggage) into a relationship.

Instead of viewing oneself as damaged goods, we should strive to accept ourselves exactly as we are. This does not underscore the need for continual self-improvement, yet it flies in the face of disowning parts of ourselves that we dislike. Accepting yourself as you are means embracing the darkness and the light – the Shadow Self. A friend of mine said something that stirred an inner realisation in the past few months. She suggested that there comes a point in a person's life when it becomes too difficult to keep up this false image of who you think you are. Rather than defend this image, it is easier to *own your junk* and embrace it rather than going to war with it. She used a poignant phrase to convey self-acceptance, *"Yes I am all those things."* She was suggesting that I am all those things which I love about myself, yet I am all those things which I dislike. How can you disown any aspect of yourself and remain at peace? I am angry, I am jealous, I am anxious, I am self-critical, yet I am loving, I am kind, I am at peace and I am whole.

From this perspective, I can be all these things and remain whole and perfect. To focus only on my imperfections underscores the uniqueness of my other qualities. By focusing on my weaknesses, I give them energy and power over me. I am choosing to identify with my shortcomings, rather than see them as one aspect of my being. As I embrace them they meld into the light of my being. The quote, *darkness is the absence of light* highlights the wholeness of who we are – loving, eternal spiritual beings. In the book, *The Deepest Acceptance*, author Jeff Foster reminds us of this truth, *"Deep acceptance always destroys our false stories. What you really long for is a deep intimacy with your own experience – the deepest acceptance of every thought, every sensation, every feeling"*. The only way to create deep intimacy is through complete self-acceptance and integration of your being – rather than going to war with it.

You go to war when you attempt to disown parts of yourself that you dislike. Liberate yourself from this unworthy cause by viewing it from the perspective of wholeness. An apple is still an apple despite its flaws, imperfections and discolourations. A carpenter working with wood will remind you of the uniqueness of the material, highlighting the imperfections in the wood's grain and texture as a desirable quality. Own your own story, embrace your experiences and live your truth. Freedom is attained the moment you accept yourself as you are – not as who you think you should be. It is liberating not having to defend one's image any longer. Drop the image and persona by embracing the mantra, *"Yes I am all those things"* as the bedrock of your being. You are yin and yang, you are winter and spring, you are light and dark. Without these elements how would you experience the contrasts of life? Allow this truth to meld into your soul so that you can rewrite a new script for your life.

Complete Acceptance

It is important that we learn to make peace with our past if we are to create a new and compelling future. This does not mean that what happened to you is forgotten or swept under the rug. What has happened has already been done so you have experienced the painful moments from that situation. Yet to carry that pain into the present moment means reliving your past without beholding to the moment.

Have you noticed that people who are stuck in the past constantly talk about yesterday and how life is unfair. They feel and act like the victims that they have allowed themselves to become. Life looks to you to see who you are becoming within each moment. You are the barometer and monitor for your life. The universe simply responds to your will and intent and matches it accordingly.

If you wish to write a new script for your life you must cease to identify yourself as a victim. Victims never heal – they simply carry their scars with them throughout life, using them so that others will feel sorry for them. This brings attention to their plight that they are wounded - *treat me like wounded person.* Carrying around the wounded title is tiresome and soul destroying. It robs the mind, body and spirit of energy as opposed to joy, happiness and inspiration, which gives life to the body and soul. Therefore, one must make peace with the past and you do so by firstly recognising that all your actions, thoughts and deeds were carried out with a level of awareness that was apparent to you at the time. In essence, you acted as best as you could, given who you were at the time. As you attained personal growth and the accompanying life experiences, you were able to see the error of your ways with the aim of not repeating them in the future.

As we approach the past with an open and compassionate heart, we allow a healing energy to permeate through our past experiences. This becomes the first step for reconciling with our past. Everyone has made mistakes in their lives, no one alive today can claim to have led a perfect life. The purpose of our mission in life is to learn, gain a level of understanding and growth and use these insights to become a better person in the hope of influencing those around us. I heard the Dalai Lama proclaim to lose his temper at times and become angry – after all, he is only human. We should be concerned if he did not lose his temper, since that would reveal that he bottles up his rage. However, as he has so succinctly put it, he, the Dalai Lama, does not hold on to anger for long. He sees the emotional energy of anger as something to be processed rather than transformed into physical energy. You have no doubt heard the passage, by the Buddha who reminds us that, "*Holding on to anger is like grasping a hot coal with the intent of throwing it at someone else; you are the one who gets burned*". Accepting yourself as you are becomes an exercise in self-compassion that is forgiving your past with openness and an attentive heart. As we honour this process with ourselves, we invite a healing energy to ignite within, much like lighting a candle. It burns slowly, yet it can never be extinguished as it becomes the light leading you home back to your authentic self.

In a similar vein, if we believe there is something wrong with us, this thought alone becomes the source of further problems and must be attended to. To believe that you are less than whole is an error in your thinking. Repeatedly regurgitating this thought discolours and clouds your true persona as soon enough, you will have taken on this image of yourself as truth. You begin to identify with the error of your ways rather than see an opportunity to create a new story – a more compelling and powerful story. You are not the sum of the negative thoughts you believe about yourself. You have simply chosen an inaccurate thought context based on external evidence at the time and used that to substantiate your self-worth.

Your subconscious mind is always eavesdropping on your predominant thoughts – whether they are favourable or unfavourable. As the subconscious listens in, it receives notes on your thoughts as instructions. Therefore, when you pose the question to yourself, "I am so clumsy, why do I always make the same mistake?" it receives this in the form of a question, which it sees fit to answer. It might instruct you that you are clumsy and make the same mistake because you are not attentive to the present moment and your thoughts are carried into the future or the past. It is a call for your thoughts to stay present and grounded in the moment since your body is always in the present.

Being attentive to the moment is achieved through a state of awareness. Become aware of your breath or use of mindfulness to let go of those habitual and incessant thoughts that occupy space in your mind. Your subconscious will continue to process your predominant conscious thoughts. It is estimated that 70% or more of the thoughts we entertain on a daily basis are the same ones repeated from previous days. We rarely think new thoughts.

As you accept yourself as you are, you begin to see that you are not even your body and if you identify with purely your external façade, then if you become ill or age, are you any of these things permanently? No – you are an eternal being whose soul occupies a body that is subject to ageing and illness. Stephen Hawking, whose health condition deteriorated over the span of a decade as a result of the progressive Lou Gehrig disease, has not allowed his physical condition to define him. He has great success in popular science as a theoretical physicist and cosmologist, notwithstanding the success attained as an author of many publications.

He is but one of many people globally who have refused to identify with their physical disability, and in many cases, these people have sought to campaign against popular opinion toward disabled people. Accepting yourself entails being mindful of your faults and insecurities. We all have faults and insecurities, since this is part of the human condition. The aim is not to dispose of your faults or weaknesses, rather it is to integrate them into the wholeness of your being. Integration affirms that you are already whole and complete as a spiritual being. As you let go of the false image of who you think you should be, you make room for the person you really are.

These aspects of your character should not obscure who you are, rather they should complement you, since they become a call to transform your weaknesses and insecurities, thus becoming the foundation for personal growth and triumph. Self-acceptance is based on the understanding that you are not your anger, nor your depression or any other disempowering emotion which you have sought to identify with. These are transient states of being. Some states stay with you for short time, while others are gifted to you for a longer period and may become your soul's calling in this lifetime.

It is vital you appreciate that you were neither born depressed nor angry, these are states of being that are acquired or learned throughout your childhood and adult life. In many cases, people take on the persona of an angry person in the form of an archetype. They play this role so well that it becomes a powerful persona to disconnect from as time goes by. At this stage, many will try to separate themselves from their persona by adopting the opposite role in the hope that the angry persona vanishes. Yet this becomes the root of one's suffering, since you cannot destroy a persona that is inherently alive within you. You are the one that gave it life, whether you acknowledge it or not. You are the one who continued to feed it with thoughts all these years. The ego will not allow you to destroy it. It has too much of a vested interest in keeping you alive and maintaining your sense of self. To the ego, trying to destroy the self is seen as a suicide attempt so it will bargain against this proposition until which time it wins.

The solution is through the integration of the anger into the wholeness of your being. In my early adult life, I sought to separate myself from my anxiety and fear believing that it was a toxic state to be anxious and frightened. I understood that I had absorbed this persona from those around me and made it my own. As I continued to push against my anxiety and fear, it grew bigger until the point it overwhelmed me and took over my life. Suddenly, normal everyday events become a focal point to be anxious about. Being in public or driving a car riddled me with anxiety. At a conscious level I knew that my body and mind were not communicating as one, yet I was unaware at the time of how to stop the flood of emotions.

It was as if every anxious thought was accompanied by its same destructive emotion. As much as I resisted at first to not identify with this state, the anxiety always won until it overpowered me. It was not until I had had enough and reached the end of my tether that I realised there had to be a better way to interact with the anxiety. In time and through finding time for regular silence in the form of meditation and walks through nature, I realised that I was not the anxiety after all. Nature had shown me the dualistic nature of my being as I considered a different perspective to my condition at the time.

It was only through persistence that I came to merge with my anxiety rather than disown it. Unknowingly at the time my focus was to get rid of the anxiety since I believed it to be the cause of my suffering. Much like your immune system rallies to your defence to fight off an invading inflammation, my mind was attempting to do the same by fighting with the anxiety, believing it could win – oh how wrong I was.

As I merged with my anxiety I came to realise that I no longer sought to identify myself as an 'anxious' person, since this was a passing state. I could be calm as evident when I meditated or took a walk in nature, yet at times I could also be anxious. However, I did not stay in this anxious state for too long, since I knew and had experienced the opposite of anxiety in the form of peace and calm through my practices. I want you to know the same is true for any condition you presently find yourself in. Unless you are being treated by a mental health professional for physiological imbalances in your brain chemistry, your attempt to merge with the wholeness of your being, is very much a process that is waiting to be explored.

Finding a Path to Wholeness

The path to wholeness is the path to truth. It is the integration of all your human aspects under the one roof. You are not denying or repressing any aspect of yourself, but acknowledging all the elements of your nature. I recall during my early adult life working in a men's shoe store selling high end shoes. The sales representatives would often drop in to keep us up to date with the latest product knowledge relating to the shoes and the workmanship involved in creating such a masterpiece. I soon began to notice that customers often bought expensive shoes, which in my opinion were 'flawed.' That is, they had what appeared to be a slight imperfection in the leather that was visible. I was rather surprised to learn from the sales representative that this was a highly desirable quality as it captured a feature of the cow's hide in its natural state. I was informed that the animal would often rub itself against a tree or wire fence to remove insects or clean itself. In doing so, it created a scar in the hide that was translated into the leather shoe during manufacture. I find it fascinating that what to some may be construed as an imperfection is to others a desirable element.

I use this example to highlight how perceiving your flaws and weaknesses may in fact be seen as desirable by others. But beyond relying on others to see you in a favourable light, you must acknowledge your uniqueness first so as to become a beacon of light to shine onto others. But how do we get past the disempowering beliefs and thoughts which have invaded our mind? I affirm that as we let go of the image of who we're supposed to be, we allow the authentic person to emerge. Now while the authentic person may still be in the making and a rough cast not fully developed, you have managed to step into your own power by living your own life, not the lives of others. It takes courage and inner strength to be who you are, especially in a world that wants you to be anyone other than yourself.

Certainty remains one of the most challenging aspects of revealing your authentic self. We want to be certain that we are living our lives in congruency with our highest nature, but how do we know that we are doing so. What is the measure to gauge our progress? Regrettably there is physical confirmation in your reality other than how you are feeling within each moment. If living by your highest and authentic state allows you to feel empowered and in command of your life choices, then you are on the right path. Continue down that path to see where it will lead you. In his book, *The Undefeated Mind*, author Alex Lickerman, MD reminds us to confront our obstacles so as to draw a path through adversity where we attain inner freedom, "*Yet victory over the obstacles that confront us isn't as much about liberating ourselves from adversity as it is about obtaining the greatest benefit possible as a result of having encountered it*".

The great mystic Joseph Campbell and the imminent psychologist Carl Jung proposed that in many ways we adopt the persona of an archetype as a protective shield – *innocent, hero, caregiver, explorer, lover, sage* etc. They reasoned that this persona resides in the collective unconscious and is tied to one's core values and personality types.

Removing the mask by connecting with your core self allows a fundamental shift towards unification rather than separation. There are two questions which echo the complexity of this ideal, so allow me to clarify.

How do we get connect with the essence of our core self?

The core self is the spiritual essence of your being. It is grounded in the understanding that at the deepest level, you are more than the physical self with thoughts and emotions. These are features which allow you to interact with your physical environment, yet they do not define you. Your thoughts and emotions are fleeting states that come and go like the ocean tides. It is unreasonable to attach yourself to them since they are transitory conditions. You may be angry today and at peace tomorrow – therefore, how do you choose to define yourself based on those conditions?

The core self is often buried under conditioned beliefs, thoughts and ideas of an illusory self. Suffering occurs when we strive to uphold an image of who we think we should be. We create a persona, an image or likeness of who we *have to be* in order to feel secure, loved and self-worthy. Unfortunately life may not be so sympathetic with your alignment of self and may shatter this image via a personal crisis, i.e. divorce, illness, bankruptcy etc. The good news is that when we drop this image of who we think we should be, we allow the authentic self to emerge. The authentic self does not need to be defended or upheld, since it is egoless and transcends the limitations of time. Your authentic self is not constrained to the thoughts or beliefs about oneself – it is not limited to the needs of the ego.

What if in connecting with the core self, we dislike who we are?

You cannot oppose the truth of your existence – the essence of your nature. You may have mistaken your spiritual essence with that of your egos; that part of you that has needs, wants and desires. Suffering ensues when you disconnect with the true self, since you have chosen to identify with the ego instead. Your identification with unfavourable parts of your nature are the egoic qualities which you have attached yourself to. Instead of opposing them, allow them to meld into your spiritual being. You cannot identify and experience something that you are not. You are not fear, anxiety, misery, sadness, etc. These are mere states that you have connected with. The core self rises above these states since they are transitory feelings, *I have the feeling of sadness* rather than *I am sad* may be a better way to express it. Be attentive to what you attach the prefix *"I am …."* to, since this has the power to create empowering or negative associations.

To step into your authentic self, identify less with your thoughts, emotions, beliefs, ideas and values. I am not suggesting these are not essential elements of your being, yet they stand in the way of discovering your true essence. They impede your spiritual development, since they shroud the true self from emerging from beneath the shadow of what is already there – the timeless, loving nature of your soul calling you home.

You Are Perfect As You Are

What emotions surface for you when I say that you are perfect just the way you are. Are you aware of any internal resistance or mental chatter which conflicts with that statement? You are perfect the way you are – since that's the way you are! While I don't mean to sound condescending or trivial, you are perfect, since you are the universal expression of perfection. You were born with the perfect set of genes and a mind and body that defy anything man could manufacture. Your mission is to embrace your perfection by evolving into it, emotionally, mentally and physically. Using your universal gifts, it is possible to harness the inner resolve to bring about the change you wish. You see, the universe desires for you what you desire for yourself. The wish for material possessions to fill an emotional void does not align with universal principles, unless you align yourself with the giving of service.

Your happiness lies dormant within – it seeks you as much as you seek it. In order to find this source of your happiness, align yourself with your authentic inner self in order to manifest it with ease and perfection. Your perfection and wholeness can be found in three principles that are key to accepting yourself exactly as you are.

How can the same universal force, which allows the sun to rise each morning, birds to fly in perfect orchestration, and the beating of your heart be anything less than perfect? Many of us fail to consider the miracle of these events in our lives. We tune out, unaware of the miracles that unfold before us. Observe a young child in wonder at these miracles, such as seeing an animal in a zoo for the first time. There is beauty in the unknown to children as evident by the passage *looking through a child's eyes*. My young nephew is consistently taken back by the garbage truck which passes by his home each week. He never ceases to tire of it, evident by his mother and father taking him outside early in the morning to watch the truck collect garbage.

When you appreciate that there is something greater than what science can prove operates in the universe, you undoubtedly surrender to that same force. Our minds offer so much resistance to life at times that becomes difficult to comprehend the mysterious process which unfolds perfectly and in right timing. Recall the last time you thought of someone and bumped into them in the street later that day? These have become normal occurrences for me known as SE (Synchronistic Events) as author Dr Kirby Surprise outlines in his book *Synchronicity*. I feel an inner nod when these events take place, for they are more than just coincidence.

Love is a universal mystery, one which we are unable to explain in terms of science. How can anyone prove the existence of love? Sure, you may recite the chemical reaction that takes place between two people experiencing love, but where does love reside? Is it in the human heart? Or is it within the realm of consciousness? Are we tapping into it when we align ourselves with this benevolent force? The point worth making is that there is a great deal more that humanity and science are yet to quantify and measure, however they remain prevalent in our everyday lives.

Do you embrace your own perfection or find fault in the physical aspects of your body? To embrace your perfection means to let go of the inner critic, which is constantly convincing you of your unworthiness. Why do we listen to the inner critic over the praise? In a family relationship, there may be a critical parent and yet the child will grow up to believe the views held by that parent over the nurturing one. I fell into the same trap as a child and so it has taken almost my entire adult life to see the error of my thinking and thus readjust my beliefs. To embrace your own perfection means to be less critical of yourself. People who practice self-compassion have enjoyed greater success in all areas of their life. The inner critic, whilst often having the stronger voice, is similarly the destructive voice who halts your progress in life.

The idea of perfection should not be construed with perfectionism, which are two entirely different components. Perfectionism is conferred in the ideal that nothing is good enough and may stem from a childhood tendency to please others. This supplication tends to emerge with the child seeking to please one or both parents who may have been critical of them during their childhood. This behaviour subsequently continues to manifest throughout one's adult life in order to satisfy others while appealing to them for their approval.

Embracing your perfection suggests that you are perfect as a creation of universal intelligence or whatever you wish to call it - universe, source, God or otherwise. You were conceived in the same image as this intelligence, which coordinates the orchestration of your body's vital functioning. As you begin to embrace this perfection, you open to the awareness that life itself is perfect and that it is our thinking that tells us otherwise. Our thoughts and beliefs cloud our appreciation of the fullness of life. We believe that life should conform to our needs since we believe ourselves to be the centre of the universe.

Begin to see the perfection of your cells performing their job each day, creating new cells and discarding old ones. See the perfection of your limbs, hands and feet, which serve you consistently without fail. Do you see the beauty in others or are you drawn to their outer appearances? Whilst you may be initially drawn to their external façade, with the passing of time you become acquainted with the whole person.

In recent times I have become more aware of the energy of others that is, being attuned to other people's energy, which I feel in various parts of my body. Whist I acknowledge that I am by no means psychic, my intuition or *gut instincts* allows me to be aware of other people's energy field. For example; if I meet someone whom I do not connect with, I feel a strong headache pulsate toward the rear of my head. This is also accompanied by the need to remove myself from the encounter. Alternatively, meeting someone of a higher vibration, I'm aware of lightness around my heart. I notice a tingly sensation all over, which is accompanied by a sense of warmth and familiarity.

The message is to become aware of the beauty in others, rather than perceive their flaws. I am not suggesting that if you encounter someone who may be negative, you remain in their company in order to see the beauty in them. That would be impractical as you would be doing yourself a disservice. If someone is indifferent to you, look for qualities that are favourable in that person. There's always an opportunity to appreciate something in others – even when we have to look hard. Remember, what you see in others is already apparent in you. Recognising the quality in others suggests somewhere in your awareness is the identification of the same attribute. Even if you cannot find one positive thing about them, use the following thought pattern instead of a negative one – *that person was interesting.* This creates a neutral observation in your mind and a useful way of seeing the world.

Wherever you are in your life's journey, be it young or old, trust that you are infinitely perfect just the way you are. Accepting this way of thinking creates more of the same energy in your consciousness. It is neither conceited nor egoic to regard yourself in high esteem. It becomes ego centred when you think yourself better than others.

Embrace yourself as universal perfection forever evolving. You are work in progress that is flawless. Allow your inner beauty and genius to manifest and in doing so, give permission for others to do the same.

Learning to Love Yourself

It is important for your personal evolution that you learn to love yourself. If you do not love yourself, it is hard to expect others to love you. Agreed, whilst humans may have many faults and shortcomings, learning to embrace all your faults is central to your position of accepting yourself as you are. Loving yourself should become your highest priority if you wish to create a remarkable future. I don't mean loving yourself in a self-centered, egotistical way. To love yourself means to embrace your uniqueness and the gifts that show up in your daily life. Low self-esteem puts the brake on your personal growth by restricting your concept of self. You may never reach your full potential if you entertain recurring thoughts of low self-esteem.

Consider the following thoughts as a guide for reconnecting with your purposeful self and developing a stronger relationship with self.

Know yourself: If your desire is for personal growth, it is vital that you come to understand yourself, and know what makes you bloom. You may be aware of a number of flaws, yet embracing them and moving forward becomes your source of courage. Listen, nobody is perfect – you may spend your entire life trying to fill an empty shoe that does not exist if you follow this line of thinking. Yes, even his Holiness the Dalai Lama is subject to the conditions of human frailty. Stand before a mirror and simply admire your reflection – do you like what you see? Some people are loath to stand before a mirror and appreciate their body. Recall my earlier example of the flawed cow hide used as leather? What is considered flawed and damaged is in fact a highly desired quality for some. Whilst you may not consider yourself as important as other people, in your life story you are the hero in your own life's journey.

Stop criticising yourself: Do you belittle yourself over small things? Whenever you make a small mistake, are you aware of the small voice inside your head reminding you of your imperfections? Criticising yourself will get you nowhere really fast. Earlier I mentioned that people who practice self-compassion have been shown to be more successful and have a healthier outlook. It is vital that you begin to associate with your positive traits instead of focusing on the negative ones. I mentioned this in a previous chapter when I spoke about assuming the role of the critical parent over the nurturing one. Be aware that you are not reliving a childhood phase of your life by reconnecting with your critical parent. Let go of your need to judge yourself and move towards a state of empathy.

Embrace your positive nature: When you entertain positive thoughts, you become kinder towards yourself and your self-love and self-esteem increases. Kindness towards others becomes an expression of your self-love. You can only give out what you hold in your heart. Therefore, if you believe you are undeserving of attention and kindness, you will likely withhold sharing these virtues with others. Every person is born positive, it's simply their environment which shapes the person into a bitter individual. Even at this stage, you still have a choice to embrace your positive nature. Nothing is carved in stone unless you give it power and permission.

Acknowledge your success: You might not have succeeded according to your terms and definition, yet the definition of success is arbitrary. What does success look like to you? There are many people who never make any effort to step out of their comfort zone and yet insist that success pave a path to their front door. If you made a direct effort toward pursuing something you desired, but were unable to succeed due to any number of reasons, do not let that impair your definition of success. Failure is part of the process toward reaching your goals. In fact those who succeed in life will have you know that they failed miserably on many occasions prior to reaching success. Your success is determined by how you bounce back from your failures and lessons acquired along the way. Making an effort is a big thing. It is not always about winning, sometimes it's the effort that counts.

Release your worries: Worrying is a futile emotion that can be better spent by taking appropriate action. Worrying uses up vital emotional energy which instead can be channelled into developing emotional resiliency and fortitude. The more you entertain worrying thoughts, the more you establish a place in your mind that becomes habituated to the worrying thoughts. There is a term used in psychology known as the Hebbian theory, which states, *"nerves that fire together, wire together"*. As you continue to entertain worrying thoughts, you establish stronger neural connections in the brain for the worrying to exist. Set your worries aside since they may be holding you back from prospering at greater levels. Surely you want to taste success and transform your worries into empowering emotional energies, which can serve your greatest potential.

Forgive yourself: We all make mistakes at some point in our life – some people make more than others, yet that does not qualify you or them to think less of oneself. Holding on to your mistakes by thinking negatively about yourself inhibits vital neural pathways in the brain from learning. Your brain is engineered for growth and learning within the context of a fun environment. We are all subject to making mistakes – no one is immune to it. Learn to forgive yourself by practicing detachment of the outcomes. Trust that whatever happened in the past was done so with the level of awareness that was apparent to you at the time. In other words, you were doing the best you could given the resources available to you at the time – thus forgiveness opens the door to moving forward. Appreciate the lessons gained from your experience by seeing it as an opportunity to gain the emotional resiliency to fight other battles in life, of which many will surely be presented to you.

Be grateful: There's a good chance if you're reading this book on an e-reader or physical book, you have every reason to be grateful. If you have access to a computer you are privileged enough to have electricity, which means you live an industrialised country with suitable resources. Almost three billion people on the planet right now are living below the poverty line and it is expected that this figure will rise over the coming years. At the time of writing this book, the world's population is 7.21 billion people.

Less than half of the world's population gets by on less than $2.50 a day. Without turning this into a sermon on why you should be grateful, it is worth appreciating how much we have to be grateful for when we consider those numbers. Gratitude entails being thankful for what you have right NOW. It does not mean being grateful in the future when you acquire something of value or have someone in your life who will compliment you and become the source of your happiness. It means recognising what you have in your life at this moment is a result of the thoughts, beliefs and energy you have created to allow you to be who you are. You create your reality through the sum of your thoughts, habits and actions over time.

Being grateful does not mean comparing oneself to others who are less fortunate; for we are all navigating our own journey in life. People often ask me *"How can I be grateful when people are homeless and dying in third world countries?"* My reply is simply this; it is your obligation to be grateful NOT for what is happening in the world, but what is happening in YOUR world. Consider for a moment if every person in the world raised their personal vibration and thought energy to one of gratitude? The collective consciousness of humanity would expand, thus ending poverty, homelessness and other diseases and illnesses. Whilst I present a Utopian society in my example, it is nonetheless conceivable that we can make slow strides toward this possibility if we all play our part in the evolution of humanity through gratitude.

CHAPTER **2**

You Are Exactly Where You Are Meant To Be

"The secret of success in life is for a man to be ready for his opportunity when it comes" — Benjamin Disraeli

Have you ever had that feeling that things are not going to plan? You wish you had taken a different course in life? Perhaps if you got better grades at school, stuck it out at that job or stayed in that relationship, things would be better? I've experienced such feelings on numerous occasions throughout my life. My mind wanders endlessly examining scenarios I could have taken, allowing me a more fulfilling life. That type of thinking, however usually shows up when I am wresting with my inner self. My ego believes it knows what is best for me; oh how wrong it can be at times. The truth remains – the present moment is perfect. You are in the perfect place right now. The need to beat yourself up, re-examining how things could have been different, is ego getting its way. You chose a life path which has led you to this moment – acceptance is the first step toward fulfilment.

The Western view suggests you are in control of your life based on the choices you make. The Eastern view proposes the opposite – we are mere puppets in this purposeful universe – everything is preordained or destined. An alternative spiritual view suggests that 65% of our lives are predestined whilst 35% is wilful action. I believe a large portion of our lives are predestined; thus having wilful control to overwrite our destiny. Predetermined destiny may include such things as what family you are born into; whom you will marry (if you choose to); major illnesses; major life occurrences etc. It constitutes the principal aspects of one's life, while wilful action is being a co-creator within the overall plan.

In his book *You'll See It When You Believe It*, the late Dr Wayne Dyer states, *"You can be detached from any need to interfere in an aggressive way with anyone and be receptive to all that is surrounding you, as well as all that you are surrounding. You can stop the endless analysis of everything and instead flow more peacefully, knowing that the divine intelligence that supports your form is working perfectly and that it always will".*

Adopting this way of thinking as Dr Dyer recommends, frees you from the need to question and analyse every decision you make. You are exactly where you are meant to be right now. Your ability to change any internal or external condition is made through awareness and understanding. The ability to create your future arises through your willingness to let go of the past and how the future should be. In doing so, you allow **all future possibilities** to occur by being present and aware.

Awakening your authentic self is a call to identify with your authentic nature, by freeing yourself from distorted thinking and beliefs. These are ideas you learned along your journey to adulthood. Such thinking keeps you safe since you are less likely to take risks and get hurt. Stop fighting and resisting the present moment; whatever condition you currently face. A similar analogy may be akin to slowly sinking in quicksand. To add to further injury, you resist and attempt to fight your way out, by doing so, you are overcome by the quicksand; sinking deeper and deeper until it's too late to free yourself.

I am suggesting the universe is offering you a lifeline, inviting you to stop fighting back. She advises you to remain calm and still in order to free yourself from your self-imposed burden. When you move toward an inner helper – the knower of all things to come to your aid with all the answers you could ever need. Call on your right brain to help steer your way out of your mental prison. Your right brain is random, intuitive, holistic, synthesizing and whole. It does not speak to you in the same manner as your left brain, which is logical, rational, analytical and objective. Your right brain is where you will find the real you. It speaks to you in quiet whispers. Throw caution to the wind by listening to those silent calls from within from time to time.

Your life need not be a struggle. Your problems are opportunities if you allow them to be. Stop your destructive and distorted thinking that tells you the world should be a certain way; that life owes you something or people must fulfil your standards. Accept 'things' just the way they are; since that's **exactly** how they are. Your need to make things fit your mould is the cause of your suffering. I am not suggesting you accept less than you deserve. I suggest that you become awake and aware in order to become the **navigator** of your own life; willing to sail into any type of condition. Too often, people view life's ordeals as unwelcomed. To the enlightened, it is viewed as a gift; a valuable lesson. The lexicon *How may I use this lesson to my advantage?* becomes an empowering reflection to view your role as co-creator of your life.

So abandon your shackles by breaking free from all that holds you back. Affirm the following: *I refuse to live this way anymore. I choose to honour the greatness that is my birthright. From this moment forward I will not entertain limiting thoughts of uncertainty or doubt. I choose to live the life of my dreams; allowing my genius to shine into the world.*

Everything Happens For a Reason

The notion that you are exactly where you are meant to be arises via the willingness to accept your current life circumstances. As simple as it may sound, there is great wisdom in that passage since it contains the essence of accepting life in all her glory. Resistance leads to suffering because when we oppose life, we have constructed an inner reality, which does not match our external reality. We go to war with ourselves and the outside world believing that we were wronged somehow.

A mantra often repeated nowadays when life goes south is that *"everything happens for a reason"*. Such a phrase has become a rite of passage when life hands us lemons. If there is reason for all that transpires in our lives, what sense can we make of the universe we live in? I affirm that we live in a universe filled with infinite possibilities, simultaneously existing outside the realm of human awareness. The proverb, *"I'll believe it when I see it"* has become a common expression in popular culture. Mainstream science has taken it a step further suggesting that if it cannot be measured or quantified, it lacks scientific merit.

A great deal of what unfolds in life is beyond the realm of human intelligence. I contend that some things are best left unexplained, save adding meaning to that which is beyond explanation. Often, we are not privy to an outcome until further down the road, once the pieces of the puzzle have come together. Brazilian author Paulo Coelho poignantly echoes this sentiment in his book, *"Manuscript Found in Accra, Someday everything will make perfect sense. So, for now, laugh at the confusion, smile through the tears and keep reminding yourself that everything happens for a reason"*. Your task is to remain hopeful when outward appearances dictate otherwise. This beckons the question, how does one maintain optimism when debt collectors are hounding you for money? Or when your partner of sixteen years decides he/she is no longer in love with you? Or when someone close to you is diagnosed with a terminal illness?

In these instances it may be prudent to withhold judgement for fear of catastrophizing a situation which time is able to heal. Do not allow a temporary setback to become your defeat. There may be a greater plan taking place behind the scenes. We may not experience the bigger picture unfolding at the time. By mentally stepping back from the drama, we allow the perfect orchestration of events to unfold in due course. Remember, your job is that of co-creator acting in harmony with universal intelligence. The frailty of the human condition is that we all experience suffering and loss at some point in our lives. My father passed away from a life threatening disease many years ago and I endured my own health crisis not long after. The wisdom I gained from these experiences is that pain and suffering are unavoidable, however remaining a victim is a choice. In his book, *What I Talk About When I Talk About Running*, Japanese author Haruki Murakami reminds us that *"Pain is inevitable. Suffering is optional."*

In order to understand life, one must simply **live it** – avoid trying to make sense of life intellectually. I can assure you that any meaning you attach to an event or situation is based on perception alone. Give permission for life to flow through you. The American Buddhist psychologist, Tara Brach suggests we embrace suffering with the silent inner mantra, *"I consent"*. This powerful mantra is an inner acceptance that everything that has happened and will happen is part of life's perfection flowing through you. Your task is to remain open and receptive to energy permeating through your being without judgement. Endeavour to remain in a state of grace and reverence, irrespective of whether the circumstances are undesirable. Life does not seek your permission, it knows how to evolve without your consent. Get out of your own way and allow life to reveal herself with ease and perfection.

Many times it is our conditioned mind which prevent us from realising the gifts and perfection of each moment. Life is mysterious with its own organising system. It is our need to assign meaning to life's mysteries that cast us in despair, since we seek to define that which is indefinable. Deepak Chopra reminds us of this truth in the following quote, *"Be comfortable with and embrace paradox, contradiction, and ambiguity. It is the womb of creativity"*. The universe functions within these three components. Therefore, nothing is fixed – life is open to change and impermanence.

If you seek to attain peace of mind, let go of the need to explain life. Be open to mystery and the aspects of *paradox, contradiction, and ambiguity*. Allow space for the unexpected and non-linear to manifest. Those who are acquainted with synchronicity marvel in the joy and surprise it brings when a dear friend whom they have not thought of in years suddenly crosses their path. To rationalise it would remove the mystery and spontaneity of life.

If we accept that everything happens for a reason, suspend judgement until a complete picture of events has unfolded. Avoid assessment of a situation based on initial outcomes – trust there is more than meets the eye unfolding behind the scenes. Secondly, let go of the need to apply meaning to situations by allowing room for the unexpected. Trust that the universe functions on a timeline not of your own accord. Often, the sequences of events develop when you least expect it and may not appear in the form you had initially anticipated.

Trust that there is a greater plan taking shape in your life.

Trust In the Process of Life

Are you a worrier or a warrior? While I know that may sound cliché, allow me to give you a little insight to support the question. Dan Millman wrote a part-fictional, part-autobiographical book based upon his early life called *Way of the Peaceful Warrior*. The story tells of a chance meeting with a service station attendant who becomes a spiritual teacher to the young gymnast, Dan Millman. The attendant, whom Millman names Socrates, becomes a kind of father figure and teaches Millman how to become a "peaceful warrior".

Returning back to my earlier question. My definition of a warrior is not defined by one who engages in war – far from it. Millman refers to himself as a peaceful warrior, since his outlook on life is forever transformed as he resolves to co-operate with the forces of life, rather than oppose them. The story highlights the significance of allowing life to unfold through us. The understanding that we too can become peaceful warriors, underscores the willingness to move through life with ease and simplicity. The greatest war we undertake is waged within ourselves, since we create mental anguish when life does not go according to plan. As I mentioned earlier, there may be a greater plan for you beyond what you believe is conceivable.

In order to harness awareness of such a plan, you must learn to trust in the process of life. The following formula serves as a metaphor for allowing trust to work in your life.

Trust = Surrender + Faith

The concept of surrender does not imply apathy or inaction as many are led to believe. Surrender is a mental and emotional process of letting go of preconceived ideas, thoughts or beliefs how life should unfold. When you surrender, you allow the essence of life to expand unimpeded by one's limited perception. Faith is the kindle on the fire giving rise to trust. Without kindling there would be smoke and ash. Faith is a slow burning flame requiring time and patience to develop. One must readily make small advances in the direction of faith to yield positive outcomes. By allowing faith to serve you on a smaller scale, you collaborate with the expansive energy of life as it permeates throughout your entire being.

In his book *The Holographic Universe*, author Michael Talbot suggests there are multi universes simultaneously in existence, sometimes called parallel universes. The term multiverse has come to embody the idea that everything that can exist already does so within the space-time continuum. According to metaphysics, everything you desire is already *out there* in formless matter. All your financial, physical and relationship desires already exist within another dimension. To realise their manifestation requires that you align with the frequency and vibration of the formless energy.

What this means in simple terms is that your desires already exist somewhere, somehow beyond the physical universe. Therefore, if it is already in existence, there must be something disallowing it from making its way into your life. Right? I contend it is our thoughts, beliefs, ideas and emotional frequency which restrict the energy to become a match with our desires. It may be viewed as constructing an invisible wall between ourselves and our desires.

When you allow life to reveal herself through you, in doing so you consent to everything that happens, even if you are not aware of the complete picture at the time. You take the so called good with the bad and trust that it is serving your personal evolution. You cannot make a mistake when you choose consciously. The process of surrendering to universal wisdom invites a higher, innate intelligence to do its job without your distracting mind opposing it.

Life has a rhythm and a process of its own that may not fit in with your plans. Our minds were never intended to figure out the *processes of life*, since that remains the realm of the higher mind. Our minds are storehouses and retrieval depots, formed of memories we call upon to interpret our present day experiences. Therefore we suffer mental anguish and emotional torment when we dare to venture into that which is 'unknown.'

Trusting life is a journey unlike one you will ever experience. For many, this may be met with a sense of hesitation and trepidation. It is human nature to search for security and comfort, knowing you will not be thrown a curve ball when you least expect it. Yet life is impermanent if it is to create itself anew within each moment. Everything is subject to an expiration date and the cycles of life are indicative of this changing force.

In order to trust the forces of life, start small by venturing out of your comfort zone. While taking baby steps, allow yourself to be guided by drawing on your inner wisdom. Access your inner guidance by letting your intuition serve as a GPS, directing you to that which resonates with your deeper self. How will you know you are acting on intuition? Intuition feels right – it feels like home.

Like anything which requires practice, the more you use it the more familiar you become with the language of intuition, which is ultimately the spiritual language of your soul guiding you.

What You Resist, Persists

In identifying that you are exactly where you are meant to be and there are no mistakes in life, you have discovered that everything happens for a reason. Your past is simply that – the past. It now remains a figment of your imagination unless you continue to recall the past hurt and pain into the present moment. When you recycle the past into the present, you reignite the pain by bringing it into the present moment. The pain will continue to become stronger in intensity; as Hebbian's theory states that nerves that fire together, wire together.

If you are to move forward in life toward creating a remarkable future, it is vital to acknowledge the past by making peace with it. Making peace simply means to forgive yourself and anyone else who co-created the experience with you. It does not in any way deny you of your hurt and pain, yet to carry that pain around with you is what the Buddha describes as, *Remembering a wrong is like carrying a burden on the mind.* You are the one who has to carry the burden with you throughout life and remember the story connected to the pain.

If you were a computer that would equate to recalling all the viruses, malware and other potential threats every time you operate your PC. The computer would run ineffectively each time you booted the system, requiring you to call in a computer technician to remove the potential threats and install an anti-virus software to ward off potential threats in the future. You must be willing to move **through** the pain in order to heal. It was Winston Churchill who said, "*If you are going through hell, keep going*". The understanding is vested in the knowledge that pain and suffering are part of the human condition and serve to facilitate your personal growth and evolution. To deny the pain is to deny your growth and expansion as a person.

Resistance is a stone wall which overshadows our best intentions to thrive and prosper. We resist how life should unfold, since we are caught up in a mental and emotional battle to make sense of reality. What if I told you there's another way? What if your suffering was transformed into an empowering state when life does not go according to plan? What if instead of waging battle against the currents of life, you simply went along with it? Allow me to expand on these statements in some detail.

In his book *When Everything Changes, Change Everything*, author Neale Donald Walsch offers us the wisdom that life is our soul's calling towards its own self-discovery. Those untoward events serve not to punish you, but to reveal your deepest wisdom. To the inexperienced mind, a speeding ticket or a relationship breakup may be perceived as an unfortunate event. To the awakened mind it is a call to unlock your greatest potential, longing to be discovered. You did not come here to live a mundane life fuelled with troubles. You have choice, power and freedom to choose how you respond to life. Granted, we have very little control how the forces of life act upon us. Yet we have control in how we respond to those events which shape our life.

Your awareness towards unwelcomed circumstances continues to persist until you have acquired the lesson or changed your internal response to it. It was Dr Wayne Dyer who said, *"Change the way you look at things and the things you look at begin to change"*. There is power in choosing one's reaction to life, rather than becoming a victim to it. As you know, victims never heal. You no doubt have heard the passage that *a watched pot never boils*. Derived from a quantum physics phenomenon called the Observer Effect, put simply, it refers to changes that the act of observing will make on a phenomenon being observed. In quantum mechanics an electron changes it location once it is observed.

Translated into layman's terms; when you observe something undesirable, at a quantum level the unfavourable event continues to manifest due to your observation of it. The act of observing disallows electrons to move freely, thus impeding universal intelligence to flow freely. The universe does not have a vested interest in actions, which are deemed good or bad. If you receive a speeding ticket for reckless driving and are concerned by it, merely changing your perception and behaviour is enough to warrant a shift in circumstances – nothing radical about this idea. Another useful analogy demonstrating the Observer Effect states that if a trees falls in the forest, does it make a sound? If there is a person standing by watching the tree fall, then yes, since it is registered by his or her nervous system.

Drawing on the previous examples, it is my intention to make clear that the act of observing is a powerful phenomenon bound by the laws of physics. Spirituality takes it a step further suggesting that when you are attached to an outcome, it impedes the creative process. Detachment then should be a spiritual goal for every individual. Detachment refers to not having an expected outcome of how an event or circumstance should unfold. This is the domain of universal intelligence.

Speaker Byron Katie, the creator of the powerful self-discovery program, *The Work* offers the insight that reality will always trump your inner state. You cannot alter or change reality once it shows up. So if your husband forgets to take out the garbage every week despite your fervent reminders, reality would have you know that this is just the way it is. Developing anger toward your husband is less likely to change his behaviour since you are the one who suffers. Changing your thoughts however, allows you to let go of your resistance to WHAT IS and thus allow WHAT COULD BE to evolve.

As you offer resistance you invite more of the same energy in to your life. When you face the experience, you allow it to move through you like an empty cloud. In time you will come to appreciate that any thought or emotion does not have power over you. Often, experiences will continue to repeat themselves until you have mastered the lesson, since life favours your personal development. It can only do so by challenging you with circumstances that are beyond your comfort zone, thus allowing expansion of consciousness.

Give up your need to resist life by allowing it to move **through you**. Life does not need to happen **to you**. Suspend judgement toward labelling experiences as good or bad until you have a complete picture. There is always a hidden lesson contained within an experience – even the most challenging ones. Dealing with discomfort and pain may be confronting, although life is cyclical and everything must come to an end; even pain. Therefore, instead of running away from your emotions, lean into them by experiencing them fully. This in itself will transform your fear, anxiety or anger. Rise to your challenges armed with courage and persistence. Maintain the confidence that you have been presented with an experience from which to personally evolve.

You are never judged by the universe or whatever force you choose to believe in. You are merely invited to honour the process of life, since everything which unfolds does so in perfect timing and order.

Go With the Flow

Knowing you are exactly where you are meant to be and that there are no mistakes in life takes the burden of having to try so hard. It releases pressure and anxiety that you should or could be doing more. The underlying message contained within this chapter is cooperating with the forces of life. As you reflect on your life story, you are able to see that every decision, every thought and action was made with a level of awareness apparent to you at the time. There are no mistakes since the resources available to you at the time were all that you knew at that point. As you gathered more knowledge and life experiences, your point of focus naturally shifted to create more empowering decisions and experiences from which to broaden your horizon.

Let us examine the idea of flow as a way to naturally move with the forces of life, instead of opposing life. You have probably heard the expression, Go with the flow. It seems those with honourable intentions are frequently advising one to sail with the speed of life. But what does it mean to go with the flow with respect to knowing that you are exactly where you are meant to be? What is flow and how do we take advantage of being in flow?

Go with the flow means offering less resistance to the currents of life. It means practising the art of allowing rather than disallowing. For example, you might be resistant to any changes taking place in your life right now. Things may appear to be falling apart on the surface. This might be expressed as a distorted view of reality, since it represents an inaccurate view based on one's biased perception of what is really taking place. Perhaps what appears to be falling apart is actually making way for the new. It has been said that nature abhors a vacuum. The old and new cannot coexist simultaneously. Therefore, an aspect of your life must recede in order to allow something better to fill its place. I have come to appreciate that chaos is an essential part of the change process. Tension often occurs prior to a big breakthrough. It might be helpful to think of chaos as *ordered chaos*. Ordered chaos may be defined as a disorganised process leading to a significant breakthrough.

According to the book *Flow: The Psychology of Optimal Experience, author Mihaly* Csíkszentmihályi suggests that flow is a state of being measured by one's state of consciousness. He proposes that we have an amount of control in how we choose to interpret external events. He highlights examples of those who have been imposed with misfortune, by demonstrating how they chose to create meaning amidst the adversity. It must be noted that there is a distinction between the concept of 'flow' and flowing with life. Yet the two can exist simultaneously. When we achieve a state of flow, as *Mihaly* Csíkszentmihályi suggests, we experience a state referred to as optimal experience. The longer we are in flow, the higher the state of consciousness is experienced. Those who experience flow include; musicians, athletes, dancers or anyone tied to their passion.

Returning back to the flow of life. As we become accustomed to stepping back from the mental drama, we allow reality to permeate. This requires courage, as often we are not privileged in knowing the final outcome, and that in itself may be terrifying. However, what may appear fearsome on first impression may become a blessing in disguise and your greatest learning experience. I find surrendering control of how life should unfold amid the backdrop of drama and uncertainty, valuable for maintain perspective. I relinquish the need to control life's outcomes as ultimately I have very little power in how life develops. You cannot influence the forces of life. Often, one cannot even control their external environment let alone their thought process. Life is continually subject to change in order for the universe thrive and expand.

Have you noticed how life has its own rhythm and momentum? Personally I can find it too slow at times. Frustration ensues when I wish for certain processes to unfold faster than they do. Nevertheless, there is a greater purpose for the speed at which life evolves. Rather than oppose these forces, it is worthwhile cooperating with them. If we merely slowed down to the speed of life, there would be less inner suffering and emotional turmoil. All our needs would be met if we acknowledged the universal energy coursing through us. This often means getting out of our mind and into our hearts. Going within means tuning in to your heart's desires. When there is mental chatter, the language of the heart is drowned out by the drama playing out in the mind.

The egoic mind has a need to be heard. In contrast, the heart expresses itself in silent whispers. The egoic mind clings to events and circumstances in order for it to survive. Break for a moment to become acquainted with the language of the ego. You will find it is vested in the need for "more," "not enough" or "missing out." These are some of the ways it uses to communicate to you. It advises you if your needs are not met, you will be unhappy. Although you are likely to be unhappy regardless, since that which is attracted to you may not meet the expectations we have on the inside. It becomes a futile battle waged against your deeper self and reality – how can you triumph? By tending to your inner world with gentleness and compassion, your external reality harmonises with your inner domain. You have heard it said that your outer world is a reflection of your inner world.

I am not suggesting we abandon our goals, dreams or ambitions. Rather, occasionally it may be worthwhile to *roll with the punches* by allowing what needs to happen to do so with minimal interference. Life knows all and sees beyond the scope of our limited senses. A good starting point to go with the flow is learning to transform your worries, fears and anxieties. These lower emotional states feed off one another. The more energy you give them, the greater the emotional intensity. Transforming these energies into higher emotional states allows you to make peace with them, by attending to the messages the emotions are trying to convey. There is a hidden message contained within every experience. Delve deeper to discover what that message is to see there is a profound learning experience waiting to greet you.

CHAPTER 3

Your Past Does Not Define You - It Shapes You

Living Fully In the Present Moment

It's being here now that's important. There's no past and there's no future. Time is a very misleading thing. All there is ever, is the now. We can gain experience from the past, but we can't relive it; and we can hope for the future, but we don't know if there is one. — *George Harrison*

In the previous chapter we examined the notion that you are exactly where you are meant to be owing to the decisions and choices made throughout your life. I offered you the idea that everything happens for a reason and it is the meaning which you assign to the circumstances of your life that dictate the level of freedom you attain. As you learn to trust in the process of life, by surrendering all attachments to outcomes, events and people, you gain the inner wisdom to trust that life is forever serving you in the background. There is no need to oppose life since you are merely opposing WHAT IS. I capitalised the previous two words to draw your attention to fixed reality. I mentioned the Byron Katie's profound self-examination process titled, *The Work* which becomes the gateway to examining your thoughts rather than reacting to them.

In this chapter we will examine the idea that your past in no way limits your potential to create a compelling future if you do not allow it. I will highlight a number of key ideas that suggest that everything you experienced in your past, whether favourable or unfavourable, served to facilitate your personal expansion. Every lesson and experience, whilst unbeknown to us at the time, contains the seed of something greater if we allow life to work though us. Working through us simply means getting out of own way and letting whatever needs to happen do so without offering resistance to the process. It means suspending judgement, knowing that all will be revealed in good time if we simply let go and allow.

Have you ever experienced a mental state in which your mind fluctuates between a stressful thought about a future event, while simultaneously recalling a thought from the past? You find yourself caught in a vice-like grip buried between two thoughts which hold you captive. You abandon all hope of staying grounded in the present moment, despite your best intentions to let go of the incessant thoughts.

The above scenario is an all too familiar scene in our lives. Our minds are habitually consumed with thinking and analysing, not to mention the accompanying emotions which drive our thought patterns. In his book *A Whole New Mind*, author Daniel Pink reasons that the future will belong to the "right brain" thinkers who think in whole terms. The right brain is considered to be complete, integrated and holistic while the left is logical, analytical and objective. Living fully in the present moment invites you to draw on your right brain, which is the seat of intuition. The importance of leaning toward right brain thinking allows the integration of our sixth sense, intuition. This faculty or subtle knowledge weaves itself throughout our life, allowing us to reconnect back to the importance of being grounded in the present moment.

You may have heard it said that the past and the future are merely illusions, since they do not exist in the NOW. Where are they? The past is a memory in your mind and the future has not arrived yet. Yet we continually replay aspects of our past, whether consciously or unconsciously and bring it into the present moment. Our interactions with others are referenced by past conditioning. If a friend does not return a phone call, you may feel hurt, angry and betrayed, even though there may be a logical reason for him not calling. Unconsciously we are quick to jump to the conclusion that we have been treated unfairly. Our unconscious mind swiftly recalls the past hurts by creating the accompanying emotions. This all happens in a split second as we fall victim to our self.

In his acclaimed book *Way of The Peaceful Warrior*, self-help author and speaker Dan Millman reminds us of the importance of staying grounded in the present moment, "*The time is now, the place is here. Stay in the present. You can do nothing to change the past, and the future will never come exactly as you plan or hope for*". In order to create a remarkable and compelling future worth looking forward to, it is vital that you learn to be centred in the moment. Those who live in the past invite mental stress, disguised as regret, fear and anxiety. Similarly those who are future - orientated live with fear, worry and anger since they anticipate a future which never arrives as planned.

A well-known aphorism states that your body is in the present moment, so should your thoughts be. This is what is meant when one talks about the mind-body connection – integrating the mind and body so they are in harmony and union with one another. Mind and body cannot be united if your thoughts are anywhere but in the present moment. It is widely accepted that those who live in the past or future surrender their personal power, thus reducing the capacity to create their ideal life circumstances. Opportunities are lost since they are wishing for things as they used to be or hoping that life will unfold in a certain way. Their minds are caught up in a battle yearning for something more. As we know from Dan Millman's quote, the future never arrives as we plan or hope for. It stands to reason that we attend to the present moment with deep attentiveness.

Whilst it is easy to espouse the virtues of living in the present moment, it is a challenge to keep our attention focused in the now, since we are continually responding to our thoughts. Such thoughts would have you know of your opposition to this moment. These thoughts, in the form of the ego, instruct you that the present moment does not live up to what you imagined it to be, so suffering ensues.

So what can you do about it? How can you live fully in the present? Firstly, learn to witness your thoughts with an open heart and through the seat of self-compassion. Many people upon noticing their thoughts are out of control respond unkindly. Do not attempt to silence your mind since that only agitates it. Witnessing means observing without creating a dialogue to support the thoughts. An effective way for reconnecting with oneself and to the present moment is to draw your attention to your breath. Remember earlier I spoke about the mind-body connection? Integrating your thoughts with your body sensations allows you to be present and aware. You are shifting your attention away from the incessant thoughts into your body. Close your eyes and focus your awareness on your nostrils. Do not allow any other distractions to enter your mind. Focus on breathing in and out through your nostrils for five breaths. Do this as often as you need to throughout the day when you find yourself stressed for no apparent reason.

The practise of mindfulness allows you to reconnect to the present moment. Mindfulness aims to tame the mind through focussed attention. So that a simple act of doing the dishes can be a rewarding experience. Of course it takes practice and patience to become mindful, yet the rewards are certainly worth it.

Your Challenges Are Your Lessons

Now you understand that staying present and grounded is the gateway into mindfulness and inner peace, I wish to outline how your challenges in the past form the basis for future growth and inner expansion. Recall that earlier that I spoke about how everything happens for a reason and oftentimes that reason does not become known to us until further in the future? I also suggested that you suspend judging the experience until all the prices have come together, since you may be forming an inaccurate view of reality based on some of the parts rather than the whole.

The following story illustrates that often what we perceive as life opposing us, is merely an invitation to move through the obstacle. Winston Churchill's earlier quote reminds us that if we are going through hell, then we keep going. The understanding is that we completely engage in whatever force is acting upon us and not oppose it. To feel your suffering by becoming it liberates you from having to struggle and wage an inner battle against your outside conditions. Life can be trying so why add to the burden through self-imposed inner suffering as well?

Earlier I mentioned the work of the American Buddhist psychologist, Tara Brach who advises that we embrace suffering with the silent inner mantra, *I consent?* There is great merit in that knowledge since this becomes our yielding to the forces of life. It is in yielding, much like a supple tree whose branches sway with the wind, rather than stand firm that we allow life to permeate through us. Power is attained by yielding to life rather than resisting it. Resistance creates more inner struggle since you feel that life is unfair and that you do not deserve to be going through this turmoil. You wish the experience would pass through you and be done with, so you may return to the comfort of your daily life. Life's challenges can move the ground beneath your feet so that you feel helpless and scared. I suggest that you avoid cowering from such an experience by leaning into it instead – that is where courage is found and inner growth is realised.

I am reminded of the story of Goliath who challenged King Saul of Israel to a single combat with one of his finest warriors. Many were terrified of Goliath owing to his enormous stature, standing at six foot nine. Many of the king's soldiers were opposed to engaging him in combat fearing for their lives.

David, a young teenager, offered to fight Goliath believing he could overcome the gargantuan warrior. The king hastily refused believing he was no match for Goliath, but ultimately conceded due to pressure. And so David confronted Goliath with the most meagre of weapons: a slingshot and a few rocks. Before waging battle against Goliath, David retreated into solemn prayer to guide him against his formidable rival. With exact precision David directed his stone slingshot toward Goliath's head, killing him instantly, Goliath thus falling to the ground to be pronounced dead.

The story of David and Goliath depicts the extraordinary strength all of us possess against mightier forces. The parable from the Bible's First Book of Samuel, illustrates the impending power of man to overcome herculean forces if the motivation is compelling. The tale conveys the knowledge that our challenges are not always as they seem. In many ways we feel a close association with David as we wrestle with the forces of life. The challenges in your life are there for a reason – to guide your personal development.

So how do you remain resilient when life offers you lemons? Surely positive thinking alone is not enough to overcome the ravages of life?

Yield To Your Challenges

Accepting that life can be challenging at times, allows us to surrender with an affirmation of complete acceptance, rather than suffer. Saying yes to the circumstances that transpire in no way underscores their impact on your life. It is merely an inner declaration that everything will turn out alright in the end. It is in no way conceding in apathy as you might believe. Challenges are an invitation to accept change in your life. More often than not the changes occur gradually over time or if you are unaware, rather precipitously. If there is resistance to the change, suffering is brought on from your unwillingness to embrace what unfolds.

You would agree that life is subject to constant change. What unfolds during the initial stages of a significant life change may not be in agreement with what you had anticipated. Hence, it is the uncertainty of the change which leaves you gasping for breath, rather than the change itself. As I mentioned earlier, your response to embracing life's challenges is to lean into them with compassion and an open heart. Remember, your resistance creates more resistance, thus leading to more suffering. Leaning in to your challenges is a mental and emotional confirmation to yield to the resistance by embracing what develops.

Lessons In Overcoming Challenges

Now you might be inclined to think, "How can I accept bankruptcy and the loss of my possessions as an important life lesson? Where is there growth in that experience?" Allow me to use the following examples to illustrate how growth is possible amid the backdrop of unrest.

"In the early 1990s Neale Donald Walsch suffered a series of crushing blows—a fire that destroyed all of his belongings, the break-up of his marriage, and a car accident that left him with a broken neck. Once recovered, but alone and unemployed, he was forced to live in a tent, collecting and recycling aluminium cans in order to eat. At the time, he thought his life had come to an end." (Burns, 2003)

Neale's life-changing experience was to become the catalyst for his awakening and he became one of the world's most notable spiritual authors. His book series *Conversations With God* have gone on to sell 7.5 million copies worldwide and have been translated into thirty-seven different languages. German-born spiritual writer and speaker Eckhart Tolle also endured a similar fate at the age of twenty-nine. Having undergone long bouts of suicidal depression, he experienced an inner transformation before going on to compose his acclaimed spiritual teachings. His notable book *The Power of Now* also sold millions of copies worldwide, becoming the catalyst for ushering a change in human consciousness.

What is clear from these examples is that in spite of their misfortune, both men conquered life's plights by embracing the lessons held within their experience. Their accounts represent a show of incredible transformations in the lives of ordinary people. It must be appreciated that there is no permanency to life, even our thoughts and emotions are subject to fluctuations on a daily basis. Accordingly, your challenges are not as enduring as you might consider.

Therefore, allow your challenges to lead you without struggle. Simply uphold a quiet YES by consenting to the forces of life to take you in the direction of where your personal evolution advances. What we think we need and what is best for us are two distinct components. Surrender the need to control outcomes by allowing the goodness of life to permeate through you. You are the expression of life – do not ask what life has to offer you. Rather, what can you offer life as an ambassador for the collective consciousness of man? In this way you can see that your struggles need not dominate your response to life. Life serves to aid your growth. There is a process to life which we cannot comprehend with our conscious minds, for our minds are accustomed to thinking in terms of linear, whilst the universe functions within the container of ordered chaos.

Knowing that your past shapes your future reality, you can rest in the knowledge that all is working out exactly as it should. Sometimes we may encounter an obstacle which seems to overpower our best intentions to not allow the past to define us. Adversity strikes in all shapes and sizes and rears itself at the most inopportune moments of our life. There are numerous lessons that adversity can teach us if we allow the lessons to serve as signposts towards potential growth.

We must strive to become attentive to the lessons, whilst not allowing ourselves to become victimised by adversity itself. Otherwise we risk falling victim and become stuck in a vicious cycle of suffering, feeling life is against us. Such people never overcome their adversity, rather they internalise a story that is one of a wounded person. They replay this story constantly and soon enough they are living out the drama which they have created in their minds. Life catches up to their internalised story.

Overcoming Adversity

I want you to consider the following questions as we explore how to overcome adversity on the road to allowing the past to shape your future. Do you ever think of your problems as unending? Do you feel your adversities are pulling you backwards? If so, you are not alone. Recall earlier I mentioned the Japanese author Haruki Murakami who reminds us that *"Pain is inevitable. Suffering is optional"*. Only you can decide the level of pain and suffering to bear upon yourself – suffering is always optional. The following thoughts will allow you to transform your hardship into a positive experience if approached with an open mind and soft heart.

Adversity Is an Indication, Not a Cause

If you are constantly encountering adversity, it is a sign of a deeper problem. You may have recently lost your job and are finding it devastating to deal with. Have you taken time to reflect on what particular circumstances led you to lose it? Did you choose the right career in the first place? Similarly, if a loved one is sick, understanding the root cause of the illness empowers you to take decisive action. Are you leading an unhealthy lifestyle? Is your environment the cause? Or is it simply your attitude? Much like physical pain is a sign of an underlying issue which warrants your attention, your hardship is a sign of a deeper problem that needs to be addressed. Even though your foremost priority is to take care of the problem at hand, it is vital to unearth the root cause of the adversity in order to transform the pain. Until you deal with the root of your problem, you will continue facing similar situations.

Adversity Teaches You Valuable Lessons

We all lead fast-paced lives amid the backdrop of inner restlessness and strive to attain more happiness. We rarely pause to appreciate the people in our lives. Adversity often reconnects us to the treasures we overlook in our daily life. Such treasures are more important than money and other material possessions and include your family, friends and health. Unexpected financial loss is a call to appreciate that money should never form the basis to one's happiness. In a similar vein, illness helps you appreciate the importance of good health and disciplined lifestyle choices. An unexpected loss of a family member allows you to value the birth cycle of death and life. Whilst on the surface these things might seem superficial, it is important to learn from your challenges in order that your problems do not overshadow your life. After all, who wants to live their life running away from problems that will eventually catch up with them? Life is to be enjoyed, while accounting for the fact there will be speed-humps along the way, yet it need not be one struggle after the other.

Adversity as Your Guide

Many times, adversity invites itself into your life to alert you it is time to change your path. For example, when someone you love suddenly decides to leave you, it is useless blaming yourself (or that person). Your focus at this point should be to attend to the pain within with a compassionate heart and once the pain has subsided, transform the pain to empowering emotions instead.

It was Confucius who said, *"I was complaining that I had no shoes till I met a man who had no feet"*. Often we believe our pain is too much to bear until we come into contact with those who are suffering more wretched pain than ours. Only then are we able to see that our pain has come to teach us something and not destroy our life. Instead of getting bogged down in your problems, pay attention to those who happily carry on with life, despite their pain. Take a leaf from their book as it were and model their behaviour. In suffering we are often presented with gifted experiences, which illuminate our lives if we are open to receiving the message. When you glance at the greater reality, you will be glad to know how you have been treated appropriately and that all your problems were in fact blessings in disguise. We are all subject to adversity that has the potential to knock us down. The following points are to reclaim your personal power, whether it relates to life's circumstances, or your own shortcomings.

Rise Up Again – I remind of the well-known aphorism which states, *"Though a righteous man falls seven times, he rises again."* Continue to reflect on this verse when you find yourself going through a tough time with little respite in the distance. Affirm to yourself to rise again by not allowing your character to be determined by the fall.

Remember Who You Really Are – It is crucial to never lose vision of who you really are. By having the experiencing of adversity, you are not adversity itself. Do not allow the turmoil to overshadow your state of mind by owning the hardship. Certainly live it and learn from it, but do not allow it to hold dominion over you.

Spend Time with Those Who Matter – Spend time with loved ones who care about you and nurture your spirit. Avoid bottling up your pain and suffering, rather face them, and deal with them in an open manner. Sharing your problems with friends and family gives you motivation and strength. Your life's journey should not be faced alone. It is in sharing our pain that we reveal our vulnerabilities and by doing so a crack emerges, which allows the light to enter.

Discover Who You Really Are – In your lifetime, you may reach a point where you discover the essence of your being, independent of your connection to your work and other responsibilities. Today's culture is performance-oriented, that is you are deemed to only be as good as your last sale, break through, acquisition or promotion. See yourself as autonomous from your performances since these are things you achieved along your life's path. Your victories do not define you, whilst they certainly colour your life and add to the wide tapestry of who you are, they do not account for the deeper essence of your spiritual nature. It becomes important to separate your achievements from your true self, since defining your life by your performance is bound to cause disillusionment if and when your successes are no longer or change.

Avoid Dwelling On the Past – It is easy to become introspective when life challenges you. Many people retreat to the sanctuary of their inner world and get lost in their thoughts and emotions. They routinely continue to replay the script of their losses in order to make sense of the adversity. Some things in life are better left unexplained. The human brain cannot make sense of a number of life's aspects, yet we consider them vital to our sense of self. Trying to explain the love one feels towards their husband or wife is best left to the senses rather than the rational mind. Avoiding staying stuck invites you to surrender the need to overanalyse situations and instead move forward with unbridled enthusiasm knowing that life goes on, and whilst there is a reason behind everything, which transpires in life, oftentimes you may not be privy to the reasoning for a long time. Therefore, do not dwell on the past, yet look forward to a new future.

Remain Motivated When Life Seems To Be Against You

Whilst adversity can be a source of personal growth, there are moments in your life when motivation begins to wane. Life's circumstances can be overwhelming at the best of times and it is important that you know when to take time out to reconnect with your deepest self. This is the part of you which people often ignore in their haste to get by. Reconnecting with your deepest self is a call to go to that part of you and connect with it in a deep and meaningful way so as to find your bearings again.

We lose our bearings when we have disconnected with our essential self. Our goal is to remain motivated since life's trials can be too much to bear at times. It is vital that we establish a way to remain motivated when the tides are high and bearing down on us. One of the ways in which to find that aspect of self is to surround yourself with people who matter. Whilst this may sound rather straightforward, those who are close to us connect to us in a deeper and more meaningful way. There is a deeper and richer energetic connection which makes us come alive when we are in their company. Our bonds cannot be broken or severed even when we are away from such people. I have a handful of such friends whom I connect with often. In some cases, we may not communicate for a long period due to work or family commitments, yet the strong bond which ties us together is held strong by our willingness to foster a deeper relationship vested in friendship. Remember, you are the sum of the five people whom you spend most of your time with.

As the challenges begin to take charge, becoming your own motivator is crucial if you wish to thrive and create a remarkable future. Relying on others to motivate you leaves you feeling helpless to take charge of your life. It becomes empowering to sail through life knowing that whilst there may be bad times, you still have the courage and fortitude to change your conditions when it matters most. Motivation may come from within or from your environment. Life is a series of cycles which naturally have ebbs and flows. Often, you may find a series of forces acting upon you for no reason at all, leading to a downward spiral of loss of motivation. Becoming stuck at this level can be disengaging and leads to a loss of morale and spirit. Motivation may simply require that you make gradual steps toward reconnecting with your authentic self so as to harness your unique potential again.

In a similar vein, the ability to create positive and empowering mental states is essential as life becomes challenging. Avoid remaining stuck in disappointment for too long, since that serves to create more of the same state. Your mind is wired to thrive, yet similarly it will take the stimuli it habitually receives and adopts it as part of your natural thought process. Your subconscious mind does not discriminate between a good thought and bad thought since the subconscious mind does not reason in meaning. Appreciate that you are overwhelmed and take appropriate action to change your internal response to those conditions. Recall earlier in chapter two Dr Wayne Dyer's quote who said, *"Change the way you look at things and the things you look at, begin to change."* There is power in adjusting our response to challenges. They need not dominate our lives, since we ultimately have the power to respond to them. The famous Austrian psychiatrist Dr Victor Frankl reminds us of this power in his acclaimed book, *Man's Search for Meaning,* *"Everything can be taken from a man but one thing: the last of the human freedoms— to choose one's attitude in any given set of circumstances, to choose one's own way."* Let your spirit come alive through your willingness to embrace adversity – rise to the challenge instead of cowering from it.

Developing an unrelenting persistence that you will prevail in spite of life's hardship reinforces your human spirit with substance. Persistence is a state of mind. It is the hallmark of accomplishment given that persistent people push through pain. Pain refers to the setbacks and roadblocks that are apparent when ploughing ahead. One's ability to recover from failure and setbacks forms the basis for future success. Persistence acknowledges the existence of external forces continually acting on us. Such forces have the potential to derail or even hinder one's progress. The persistent person acknowledges these forces are working against them, yet focuses ahead. Persistent people have an indomitable will to succeed, having connected with a persuasive WHY? Their WHY is a deep motivator which compels them to take action despite external forces.

Behavioural psychologists have long believed that simply *showing up* is a sufficient measure towards future success. I hold firm to the belief that showing up is inadequate, since people show up every day to dreary and mundane jobs which they loathe. Whilst the body is present, their minds are on vacation somewhere on a tropical island. Showing up means being present and engaged with absolute intention and purpose. Using this analogy of showing up can be a powerful motivator for helping you overcome life's challenges. Allowing life to be what it is drops resistance from overwhelming you, thus surrendering the need to suffer. Suffering is only present when you oppose the conditions of your life, by believing there is a better way than what is actually apparent.

Similarly, it is worth considering that you do not become embroiled in negativity when life's forces act upon you. Celebrate your accomplishments by looking back to see how far you have advanced. Many people adopt the inner critic in times of turmoil, wishing they had not acted in a certain way, although self-criticism has been shown to have the opposite effect on progress. The drill-sergeant approach rarely works in such a setting since your mental and emotional brain does not respond in kind to that type of motivation. However, self-directed compassion opens the gateway to inner peace and transforms the sorrow of the past.

Where There's a Will There's A Way

As we close this chapter, I would like you to consider that history has shown there are numerous people who overcame insurmountable obstacles and setbacks to succeed. They did not allow their past to dictate their future, nor did they carry the burden of the past with them. You might even be surprised to discover that many successful entrepreneurs are diagnosed with the developmental reading disorder dyslexia, including well-known Virgin founder Richard Branson. In spite of what might seem an insurmountable obstacle, many people continue to thrive despite their impediments.

Daniel Pink author of *A Whole New Mind* cites Sally Shaywitz, a Yale neuroscientist and specialist in dyslexia who says, "Dyslexics think differently. They are intuitive and excel at problem-solving, seeing the big picture and simplifying... They are poor rote reciters, but inspired visionaries." Dyslexics have to overcome enormous odds in order to succeed, which represents their strong will to thrive. It is estimated that a number of leading international CEO's past and present are also dyslexic.

The human will is undeniably powerful. Once a stern commitment is made to carry through with a project or goal, there is very little to stop a person. You may have heard it said that the human will has the capacity to move any mountain. As long as one's will is resolute and fuelled with the right intentions, a person can overcome anything on their road to victory. Will power then becomes man's greatest ally for success. Interestingly, in Malay the title of this section translates to the following passage, *When you want to do something, you will find a thousand ways possible to achieve it; but when you don't want to do it, you will have a thousand excuses not to do it.* In this instance we see that will and intent are two powerful factors required to create a remarkable future.

The other necessary aspect is **purpose** and **passion**. Purpose may be defined as understanding one's role within the cosmos. It is the ability to harness your skills, talents and genius and direct focussed attention to a pursuit which resonates with your deepest self. A purposeful vision becomes an extension of this faculty, since it coincides with a common goal that benefits humanity. One might conclude that the union of a strong will and purpose creates a purposeful vision, clothed with honourable intentions. Many pioneers have achieved enormous success in spite of prevailing external circumstances. It was Albert Einstein who said that *"Great spirits have always encountered violent opposition from mediocre minds."*

For me, vision is the foresight to envisage an outcome without external validation. It is the ability to venture into the unknown realm; an inner knowing beyond the call of reason. Irving Stone's classical biographical novel, *The Agony and The Ecstasy* depicts Michelangelo having an undeniable vision to paint and sculpt masterpieces. He overcame numerous impediments, which included the political agendas of the papacy entrusted into power at the time. A strong and clear vision, matched with a strong sense of purpose opens up many roads and avenues to achieve one's future life path.

Those who have vision will stop at nothing to see their project come to life. Tony Hseih's is one such visionary whose commitment was to build the largest and most successful online footwear retailer Zappos. The company was subsequently sold to Amazon for over one billion dollars. Tony's executive team continually faced obstacles and setbacks along the way to building a global business. The quote, *"The bigger the goal, the harder the climb"* rings true in this case. Having established that purpose and will are vital ingredients toward living a remarkable future, the other factor which is a common thread to bind purpose and will is knowing your why? Your why? is the motivating force behind why you choose to pursue your life path. When the road ahead becomes challenging, as it no doubt will, your why? is the inner reassurance, which reminds you why you started your wish to create a purposeful life. Without a WHY? your vision lacks passion and the endurance to sustain you in the long run.

My personal WHY? is connected to observing my father struggle with health problems while he was alive. As my father developed type II diabetes during his later years, I sought to understand the mechanism underlying human illness. Many years later I would also undergo my own health crisis. My why? is a daily reminder why I choose to empower people with the message of health and self-empowerment. It is strongly tied to an emotional setting which is all too alive in my mind and body.

The final ingredient necessary for achieving a remarkable future is **determination**. This faculty matched with will and purpose is strong enough to overcome any obstacle life presents. Your determination when powerfully connected to your why? becomes the ignition which flames the fire toward lasting success. Nothing can stop a person who is aligned with the blueprint outlined below. They have aligned with their purpose and through a strong determination they connect to their WHY? and are able to achieve an unimaginable destiny fuelled with passion and purpose.

Wilful Purpose + Determination (WHY?) = Inspired Success

Those with a strong will and purpose rise to reframe failure. They see it as an opportunity to draw closer to their imagined future. It becomes a signpost rather than a dead-end. The cause and effect model which many people subscribe to dictates that if a venture does not work, one should abandon it. Yet there is something powerful about the person who labours on despite the obstacles life throws at them. I draw your attention to Thomas Edison having failed one thousand times before finally creating the electric light bulb. When there is a strong will matched with a powerful vision, failure takes a backseat toward greatness.

Before you go on to the next chapter consider the following question: **How can you reframe your current life's situation so as to infuse it with purpose, will and determination?**

CHAPTER 4

There Are No Mistakes

Embracing What IS

"There is so much division in this world. So what is really the path of healing? It can begin in this moment, by embracing the life that's here." — *Tara Brach*

In the previous chapter you discovered your past does not define you, rather it shapes you. We examined a number of ideas built on the understanding that pain and suffering can be a teacher if you allow the experience to penetrate your being. Challenges and setback are inevitable when you seek to live a rich and rewarding life. Putting yourself out there is bound to invite successes and failures – you need to take the good with the so called bad. I say so called since you do not know how a bad experience can turn into your greatest lesson if you allow it time to pass through your life.

In this chapter I wish to make a case for mistakes not existing in the universe, let alone your life. Every so called experience has served you to arrive at this point in time. If you are reading this book, then you have transcended any experience life has presented you with. How do you know this? Well you are here, alive and well and reading this book. Every experience, every single untoward event has allowed you to rise above it and discover a deeper aspect of yourself so that you could be here in this moment.

As we learn to embrace what is, we surrender the need to create our own story and drama, which we believe is better than what is unfolding in our external reality. Accepting the perfection of this present moment allows you to let go of needing to change anything out there. However, this does not mean that you surrender in apathy. It means that you now offer less resistance to the forces of life, knowing that everything taking place in your life is part of your personal evolution.

Embrace life by perceiving it as a practice, much like sitting meditation or exercise. The more you practice, the better you become. Your mental and emotional states become attuned to offering less resistance through an awareness to the present moment. The practice of embracing life means that at times you will naturally slip up. This should be an opportunity to practice self-directed compassion, instead be less critical of yourself, since you are learning a new language.

As you become better at embracing what is, you will naturally find every thought and accompanying emotion develops into purposeful action, which is met with an infinite acceptance. Resistance gives way to understanding, compassion and boundless patience. These three aspects unite to allow life to become a process naturally flowing through you. In contrast to your previous way of thinking, it may be viewed as a giant boulder obstructing the flow of a river through a brook. As the boulder is removed from the water's pathway, it naturally begins to flow in an unimpeded way. Your life circumstances may be viewed in the same manner once your resistance is transformed into inner peace.

In a similar vein, who said that life had to be smooth sailing all the time? Perhaps it is mainstream media that thrives on portraying the lives of wealthy people and celebrities leading exotic lives. Unknowingly, we buy into the notion we are missing out on living the same dream life. As fine as it may sound, we are not privy to the drama which unfolds behind the scenes for these same people, since we are only aware of what they want us to see in the glossy magazines – exotic lifestyles and not the behind the scenes drama playing out in the backdrop of their lives. Where does growth occur if there is no contrast from which to grow and experience yourself? Growth and expansion are essential to the human condition since it marks your development throughout the various phases of our life. If you were to entertain the same thoughts in your forties as when you were in your twenties, you would find your view of the world limited and subsequently your circle of friends and business acquaintances also limited. Inner growth allows us to transcend problems and in doing so expand our level of consciousness.

There are great lessons and an ongoing expansion of your awareness when you accept suffering is part of the human condition. And yet, suffering does not have to mean that you are stuck in this cycle of pain or you are a victim. There are many great people throughout history whose suffering healed not only aspects of themselves, but liberated others in the world as a result. Viktor Frankl, Martin Luther King, Gandhi and Nelson Mandela are a few who suffered difficult lives, yet managed to overcome their ordeals and go on to leave a mark on the world.

There is no need to change your current circumstances since everything exists in a state of perpetual change. Circumstances which you believe are continuous and non-changing are simply your thought processes held in a fixed state. You believe your current reality should conform to the image you have in your mind and it is this destructive thought itself which needs to be attended to and healed before you can accept life is anything but fixed. Life creates itself anew within each moment as long as you embrace the uncertainty of change as an evolving process.

Therefore, make it your task to get out of your head and into your heart. Interact with life from the level of the heart. The rational mind is not privy to information about your surroundings – your heart holds vital clues to the nature of your world. The key is to become quiet enough to listen to the silent whisper of the heart by attuning to its frequency. Embracing what is becomes an inner surrender to the wisdom which lies within. This wisdom is forever working in your favour, yet becomes drowned out by the chatter of the conscious mind, which seeks to have its own way.

Life's Greatest Lessons

Knowing there are no mistakes removes the burden from having to strive to make things happen. You learn to let go of frustration, disappointment, anger and anxiety to trust all will be worked out for your greatest good when the time is right. Universal timing affirms there is a rhythm and a cycle to life which is independent of your own timeline. What may seem as a dead-end or roadblock may actually be a blessing in disguise. Not receiving what you want may sometimes allow something greater and more substantial to make its way into your life. The challenge is we are not often privy to the behind-the-scenes details. Frustration and disappointment ensues since we feel that our desires are not manifesting as we had imagined. But timing is everything as you know.

I have witnessed it in my own life, that everything I ever wanted either made its way into my life at a later stage when I was mentally and emotionally in the right place. Concurrently, there were desires which never manifested in the form I believed them to be, since I was resisting, thus blocking the flow of universal intelligence. As I learned to let go of my attachments to outcomes and simply surrender, even greater resources made their way in to my life with effortless abandonment. In this section, I would like you to consider a number of key lessons that will serve you well as you come to appreciate there are no mistakes in life. The following principles are useful guides to consider as you create your remarkable life. As with most things, releasing and surrendering your attachment to outcomes, will yield positive outcomes, since the universe specialises in the mysterious and unexpected. Like watching a pot that never boils, expectations and outcomes also have the capacity to limit your flow of life.

I want you to reflect on what has been your greatest life lessons so far. Perhaps it was learning to love, discovering a hidden talent, being independent, not judging others, living in the moment, not taking others for granted or other notable ones. The following points are lessons that have served me well throughout life, yet came at a cost of great inner pain and turmoil at the time. Like most people, I resisted what was happening to me, believing there was a better way each time. Oh how wrong I was to think I knew better. Life, as you know is a great teacher, it gives you the experience before the lesson. Life has become more enjoyable and rewarding over the years as I slowly adopted these principles into my life.

In hindsight, I needed to have those lessons. There are no mistakes in this universe – everything is perfect and unfolds at precisely the right time and place.

Life unfolds as it should, not according to your schedule – Have you ever wished things would happen quicker? You may become impatient believing you are never going to receive your desires. You give up hope of it ever manifesting. Just when you give up, your wish appears miraculously at the right time. Looking back on the theme of my life, this is one of the most powerful lessons I have encountered. I compared myself to others in my youth, believing I was not talented or smart as other the kids. Over time, I developed many talents, which came through sheer determination and tenacity. In many cases, my understanding of concepts and ideas were deep and long lasting, since I took my time in acquiring the experience. In many instances I outperformed other kids whom I earlier compared myself to. Life had taught me to practice infinite patience and the price of valuing my self-worth.

Gratitude draws more abundance into your life – It was not until my early thirties that I began to appreciate and observe this universal principle. Practising daily gratitude, whether through meditation, emotions, journaling or otherwise, allows more of what you value to flow into your life unimpeded. Human behaviour expert, speaker and author Dr John Demartini from the movie *The Secret* reminds us, *"Whatever you don't appreciate, depreciates."* Therefore I have become grateful for the smallest things, such as loving relationships, my health, the nutritious food I eat, the job I perform and the people in my life. I allow more abundance to flow into my life since I align with positive emotions and energy, which brings forth more of the same frequency. Your emotions are a communicating gateway to the universe – it is an inner acknowledgment of thanks that everything is exactly as it should be. If you were conversing with the Universal Intelligence, the conversation might be something like, *"I'm pretty cool with all this great abundance you're sending me. Thanks, I get it and appreciate it."* Appreciation and gratitude flows from the heart. As a side note, the heart has by far the strongest magnetic field of any organ; it is 5,000 times stronger than the brain's frequency. The organisation "HeartMath" has conducted numerous studies in this area. Therefore, when you FEEL an expansive positive energy radiating in your heart area, otherwise known as the heart chakra in Eastern traditions, you radiate that goodness into the universe. The FEELING may be akin to the emotion felt when in the company of a loved one or similarly when you are feeling appreciated and loved.

The world is a beautiful and amazing place – Why? Because this should become your point of reference in choosing your outlook on reality. You choose to create any belief or image of the world as you see fit, so why not choose an empowering thought or belief and infuse it with the appropriate energy? It should not matter that tens of millions of people believe otherwise; creating an enriching reality at the level of the mind must become your primary focus if you are to move toward creating a remarkable future. Do not be dissuaded by what reality presents you with, since your present day reality is merely the amalgamation of your past thoughts and beliefs represented in the present moment. You have the power to change your future through directed attention and awareness to the present moment. Listen, I don't care where you've come from or where you're going. I don't care if you've scaled the highest mountain or swam across the ocean. I want to know about your inner world. How do you paint your picture of life from within? This is what matters. You see, for the enlightened, even disasters and tragedies are a part of the mystery of the universe. They appreciate there is a force and energy within the universe that our limited minds cannot appreciate. The world is beautiful when you suspend your ego, which tries to convince you otherwise. The beauty of life is contained within you and radiated outward, like a fire hose with great pressure – the water has no place to go, but to gush out at high intensity. I want you to regard life in the same manner; with unbridled enthusiasm and passion.

Less serves as more – You may have noticed in your twenties life was dominated by the speed of life, travel, work, play and socialising. It was about how you could travel from one destination to the next in the shortest amount of time in order to commence the next adventure. You may have missed out on the journey, which occurred in-between along the way since your focus was on the future. You may have failed to appreciate the smallest details around you. Many people report an emptiness during this period of the life. As a result depression sets in since they have convinced themselves that life is not all as it is cracked up to be. Nowadays, these same people report a meditative aspect of doing less; yet achieving more. What do I mean by less? Less worry, less anxiety, less work, less effort. Take time to observe nature and you will see the same principle working effortlessly. A tree does not force its way out of the ground to grow. When the conditions are right, it slowly and surely emerges from the soil into a beautiful tree bearing fruit and shade for other animals and people. On a personal note, as I learned to slow down to the rhythm of life, I discovered that I was able to achieve more in my life while doing less. Had I bought into the ideas of mainstream culture, I would have been burnt out, working in a job I hated and in a relationship which did not serve my personal evolution. There is a lot to be said about bucking the trend of travelling fast through life and missing all the great experiences in-between. Go with your heart – it knows best.

I would like you to reflect on what has been your most valuable lessons over the years, which still serve you well?

How have they shaped the person you are today?

Were those lessons essential for your personal growth?

Collaborating With the Forces of Life

As you begin to appreciate there are no mistakes in life and everything unfolds exactly as it should, your life begins to acquire a momentum of it is own. There is less of a need to strive, to worry and become anxious about circumstances that once troubled you. This is not to say that you become bereft of problems – rather you walk through your problems knowing that you have the inner wisdom to work through whatever life bestows on you. And even then, you realise that your problems are not as bad as you once believed and may in fact be paving the way for a deeper experience. Your soul wishes to experience life in all its contrasts. It does not view your life problems in the same way as your conscious mind would. You soul is multi-dimensional and therefore knows every possible future scenario before it exists in time and space. It knows your experiences have been orchestrated for you to advance your soul's progression.

In his book *The Seat of The Soul*, author Gary Zukav suggests this need to collaborate with the forces of life knowing that through cooperation and trust all will be taken care of, *"The fourth is to allow yourself an orientation of openness toward your life and the Universe, to approach the questions in your life with a sense of faith and trust that there is a reason for all that is happening, and that that reason, at its heart, is always compassionate and good."*

Collaborating with the forces of life entails working WITH the events and circumstances which show up in your life. It means complete resignation and acceptance that every event has a hidden meaning and blessing, otherwise it would not be happening to you. To allow collaboration to work for you, drop whatever resistance you feel toward life right this very moment. If I handed you a hot coal what would be your first instinct? Naturally it would be to drop it instantaneously so as not to get burned. Holding on to the coal increases the pain. The same is true of holding on to pain and suffering as a result of your refusal to accept life.

You see, everything that needs to show up will do so according to universal timing – there is no need to rush the process of life. The universe functions within the container of timing and order. Everything that needs to happen will do so without your need to hurry things along to conform to your schedule. You may have seen evidence of this in your own life when young. Learning to ride a bike for the first time could not have been hastened along even if you wanted it. Yet, as your body and mind developed, there came a time when you were ready to ride your bike, even though you may have had to use training wheels to help you find your way. In time though, those training wheels were removed as you found your balance and became better acquainted at staying upright on the bike.

Life has shown me this to be true in relation to swimming as a child. I was intensely uncomfortable around water, fearing I would drown even in the shallowest part of the pool. I have no recollection of where this fear originated and fought hard to overcome it in numerous ways. Yet, the fear managed to overpower me. However, one summer, while playing alone in the local swimming pool I summoned the courage to move further away from the edge of the pool in an attempt to see if I could swim unaided back to the edge. Each time I increased the distance by one meter. Soon enough I was able to swim the entire length of the pool without the fear that I would drown. Time, patience and courage allowed me to take appropriate steps to overcome my fear. I can assure you it could not have happen any sooner, even in light of my persistence and determination.

Similarly collaborating with the forces of life means your resistance will limit the perfection of life through you, since you are upholding an image of how things should unfold, instead of how they are. The American speaker and author Byron

Katie has the following to say about working with life, *"Life is simple. Everything happens for you, not to you. Everything happens at exactly the right moment, neither too soon nor too late. You don't have to like it... it's just easier if you do."* She advises us that it's just easier if you like what happens to you, rather than oppose it. If there is one central theme I would like you to take away from this book, it is this: do not oppose life, even if you feel that what is happening to you is not what you wish for. Change your internal dialogue of acceptance. I have provided you with an emotional scale down below. I invite you to note where you reside in terms of your opposition to life on the scale. Make it an effort to examine and transform your beliefs each day until you have reached the level of Love/Ecstasy. Start at the emotional level where you believe your outlook most represents your present view of life and each day make an effort to examine your thought process until you have reached a powerful level.

Scale of Emotions

- Love/Ecstasy
- Joy/Elation
- Ease/Power
- Enthusiasm/Ambition
- Hopefulness/Optimism
- Interest/Inquisitiveness
- Acceptance/Peace
- Introspection/Contemplation
- Pensiveness/Melancholy
- Indifference/Apathy
- Unease/Discontent
- Frustration/Aggravation

Confidence/Inspiration

Excitement/Passion

Anticipation/Eagerness

Worry/Nervousness

Doubt/Pessimism

Anger/Blame

Anxiety/Fear

Grief/Desolation

Despair/Worthlessness

Powerlessness/Dejection

Depression/Hopelessness

It may be useful to appreciate there is a process and evolution to life which needs to unfold unencumbered of your preconceived ideas – allow the unfolding to happen without impeding it. It is going to happen regardless, so why add a narrative imbued with negativity. Wouldn't you rather sail through life without the mental and emotional anguish that worrying and anxiety bring? You have a choice, and that choice awaits your decision to step into the acknowledgement of choosing to collaborate with life or suffer at the fate of disempowering emotional states. Choose wisely and though it will not be easy, know that what awaits you on the other side is liberation from the inner turmoil that has dominated your past life.

Release Your Expectations

As you will discover, working with the forces of life yields innumerable advantages. You will notice there is less of an attachment to outcomes, since life now flows through you. You hold no expectations of how life should unfold since you trust that it will do so in the manner that it chooses, irrespective of your mental state. There is no need to hold onto anything anymore, since you are now in a new world where holding onto things, people and circumstances only limit your experience of life. Reality has shown you that as you allow life to happen, you will always be taken care of and there is no need to worry about the future.

Consider the following Zen story depicting how expectations limit one's experience of reality:

Zen master Baizhang was walking with Mazu and saw a wild duck fly by.
Mazu said, "What is that?"
Baizhang replied, "A wild duck."
To which Mazu asked, "Where is it going?"
Baizhang said, "It is flying away."
Mazu twisted Baizhang's nose and said, "When did it ever fly away?"

Baizhang assumed the duck flying away from him was central to his experience of it. He attached meaning to his experience, rather than assume the duck was flying over him toward its destination.

The kōan has a familiar riddle which offers the lesson regarding our willingness to release expectations. Baizhang mistakenly related his experience of observing the duck in flight as central to his universe, i.e. flying away from ME. Expectations have the same effect by limiting the flow of the experience. We add layers to our experience of life in order to rationalise the world, albeit at a cost by limiting our perspective. In his first interview with Oprah Winfrey, Brazilian author Paulo Coelho, who wrote *The Alchemist*, attributes his success to being open and receptive to uncertainty. He reminds us to flow through life – allowing it to carry us where it needs to, devoid of expectations, anxiety or frustration.

As we gain trust in the rhythm of life, we acquire confidence through our attentiveness to the signs life bestows us.

Undertaking quiet time for reflection will allow you to reconnect with purpose. Are your expectations valid? Why is it important that circumstances transpire as you expect? Your answers to these questions will highlight the principal motivation driving your expectations. Often, if we surrender to universal intelligence, an even better result than we had anticipated will emerge into our experience. There is a Chinese axiom echoed by the following tale, which states; our cups (minds) are overflowing with concepts limiting our experience of life. *"You are like this cup; you are full of ideas. You come and ask for teaching, but your cup is full; I can't put anything in. Before I can teach you, you'll have to empty your cup."* In order to see past your expectations, we must become empty vessels so life may pour herself into us.

This allows us to get past the story in our minds and appreciate life for what it really is. Most people's perception of life is obscured by subconscious programs – they maintain a distorted view of reality, which discolours their experience. It should be said that no two people share the same experience, not even twins. Anthony De Mello was a Jesuit priest and psychotherapist who wrote a delightful book titled, *Awareness: The Perils and Opportunities of Reality.* In the book he outlined how our experiences of the world are tied to our awareness or lack of it. Every encounter stems from your **perception of reality** – not reality itself. He affirms we must look past the veil of illusion created by the mind. Moreover, your expectations are **mind-made illusions,** which you hope to create "out there."

How can you liberate yourself from expectations while fulfilling your human needs? Firstly, experience the world through the eyes of a child. Surrender all expectations by remaining captivated by uncertainty, which is the birthplace of creation. Secondly, stay grounded and present – this allows you to let go of future expectations and the need to recycle the past in to the present moment. Remaining present invites you to embody life's experiences with fullness. As an illustration of a distorted reality, when you view the sun you are seeing it where it was eight and a half minutes ago given the Earth's approximate distance from it. You are not seeing the sun where it is NOW, since it has moved. Therefore, everything in life is transient – if we miss the opportunity to stay grounded and present, life will instantly pass us by.

A timely quote by Krishna Sagaar reaffirms our position of a subjective reality, *"You don't see the world as it is, you see it, as you are."* Thus you do not experience reality as you believe, but through a self-made filter of your accumulated beliefs, thoughts and emotions carried over time. In addition, seek to get out of your head and into your heart. Abandon your fantasies about what life owes you. Life does not serve to fulfil your every request like an online order catalogue. The moment you engage life with purpose and passion, your expectations no longer dominate your thought landscape – all your needs will arrive precisely at the right time, when you least expect it.

Reaffirm silently that everything you need is available to you right now. Trust and release the desire to know it all. Be open to infinite possibilities by being patient and trust that your needs have always been met and will continue to do so in the future. Surrender the need to control life's outcomes – for seeking to control life is like struggling to clutch at water with your hands open.

Life Is a Beautiful Struggle

Up until now we have examined a number of ideas which suggest there are no mistakes in life. I asked you to embrace life by allowing whatever is unfolding in your life right now. Suspend judgement and do not label something as good or bad until a complete picture has emerged. We examined four principles espousing some of life's greatest lessons, some of which have formed my personal lessons and experiences. I posed the idea that collaborating with the forces of life shifted the focus off worry, blame, frustration and anxiety to one of peace, harmony and anticipation. The understanding is based in the knowledge that everything that needs to happen will do so independent of your resistance to it. In a previous section I put forward the thought to release your expectations of how life should unfold since disempowering thoughts about the future limit ones experience of life via the narrative added to it.

I would like to conclude this chapter by offering you the sense that your struggles are part of the human condition and can shape your life in numerous ways if you remain attentive to the lessons contained within the experiences. Life is either one big beautiful struggle or nothing at all. Many of you would undoubtedly wish life was without challenges or setbacks. But if that were so, how would you realise your potential without struggle? Without growth, life would be dull and dreary. We strive and struggle so that we may overcome – for it is in overcoming that we prevail and realise our magnificence.

Now you might regard yourself as just an ordinary person. Perhaps for some, the desire may be to win the Nobel Prize for scientific achievement. Nonetheless, we are all equipped with an inner calling to grow and thrive. It is inbuilt into our genetic DNA to grow into better versions of our self. As you extend yourself to become more, you join forces with universal intelligence to express your infinite potential. We play a small role in the greater orchestration of events which take place in the physical universe. This does not mean we play an insignificant role in the co-creation process, rather the decisions we make today have a ripple effect in our lives and the lives of others. We are all connected on a deeper level, since our lives are all intertwined.

Your beliefs frame your perceptions. Your perception colours your view of reality, so that what you expect is what you get – an ongoing discussion that life is one struggle after another. Yet it does not have to be that way. There is far more to life than your impression of it. Notice I used the word impression, since the way you perceive the world is marked by your observation of it. Life does not have to be a chain of endless struggle, paying the bills and being dissatisfied in one's job. The same bias of struggle is apparent toward ageing. One need only consult with a minority who believe ageing is an inevitable process burdened with a gradual decline in mental and physical ability. We fail to concede that we have the power to slow the ageing process by tending to our health on a frequent basis. Suddenly, instead of being victims to the forces of life, we have the power to decelerate the ageing process and thus live richer and fuller lives.

Life offers us moments of bliss when we least expect it. The lucky break that comes just at the right time, having devoted much of your life to pursuing your passion. Our struggles pale into insignificance when we are in love and committed to serving others. Life does not come with a user's manual – we approach things blindly, hoping they will yield a favourable outcome. I don't know about you, but I wouldn't have it any other way – the joy of overcoming a challenge or setback is rewarding and part of the human condition. Life is willing to offer you so much or so little. Life offers heartache, pain, emotional trauma and moments of anguish. This is in contrast to the delightful moments of falling in love, witnessing the birth of your child and of course personal victories. Pain exists to give rise to joy. The principle of duality, contrast and paradox work in synergistic harmony to one another – Yin energy is the complement of the Yang energy.

Life is called a journey, for it is the experiences we embark on that have a lasting effect on our lives. Life is a series of highs and lows. Those moments of bliss or episodes of agony remain a central focal point long after the experience has taken place. We should not assume that life will conform to your desires at the drop of hat. We must allow life to flow through us unimpeded. We do so by remaining receptive to what shows up; even if we believe otherwise. This has been a central theme running throughout the book which I purposely wish to emphasise. The title of this section illustrates the dichotomy which unfolds in our life. Without the drama and the struggle, life would serve no function. Through chaos life is born, which serves as the impulse for the creative expression of life itself. We see this application throughout nature. Diamonds are formed under intense pressure, heat and agitation. The turbulent weather patterns eventually recede to give way to the welcoming spring and autumn months. We look forward to these seasons rather than take them for granted. Imagine for a moment if we had one season for all twelve months of the year? There would be little to appreciate in terms of the contrasting weather changes. Contrast emerges in nature so that we may experience diverse realities.

I invite you to reframe your challenges as analogous to the seasonal changes. Nothing is permanent. Painful experiences come and go if we allow them passage through us. Rather than view life as a series of endless dramas, appreciate that all your personal battles are leading you toward the realisation of your deepest wisdom. This wisdom connects you to the same intelligence that instructs the trees to bear leaves in season. It is serving you every moment. It might not show up in the way you expect it, yet it is always working in the backdrop of your life.

Life can be a series of beautiful struggles or nothing at all.

CHAPTER 5

Make Peace With The Past

Healing the Past Is Vital to a Successful Future

"When you forgive, you in no way change the past – but you sure do change the future." — *Bernard Meltzer*

It is safe to say that everyone has a past and in that past are most likely painful memories, disappointments and frustrations. This journey of life is not guaranteed to be a bed of roses, as everyone goes through painful times. Many people cope with the negative emotions which accompany the painful experiences, but there are many that do not cope in a positive way. There is a tendency to stow the pain where it gets locked in the subconscious mind. Many do not realise they are doing this. This negative energy buried deep down may stay there for a while, but eventually it tries to surface so that it can be dealt with. It is there lying beneath the surface since emotions are simply energy in motion, which yearn to be expressed. The repressed emotion will manifest in certain ways and at certain times until it is dealt with.

Healing the past and the pain associated with it is vital to a successful future. The first thing that you must do is to recognise that you've stored your pain down deep throughout the years. The mind is astute at protecting us and unwittingly we bury the pain in an attempt to dispose of the painful feelings and emotions associated with the experience. Maybe your childhood contained dysfunctional circumstances or perhaps you were bullied at school. Perhaps you had a verbally abusive partner who attacked your self-worth. Or maybe you never accomplished what you set out to do due to fear and doubt.

I would like you to consider your past in the coming pages in the context of how you can transform those painful experiences into empowering ones. Take a day or a week — take as much time as you need. Are there things that happened a long time ago which you still feel pain or anger from as a result? Do you feel like you were victimised, criticised, abused, or neglected? Invite the negative feelings to surface so you can take an honest look at them. Feel your feelings. Yes that's right, feel the emotions which resurface but do not attach meaning to what comes. Feeling your feelings requires courage, especially if those feelings have been stowed away for years. It is critical to face your emotions head on when it comes to healing wounds and freeing yourself up for a happy future.

Victims never heal. If you have adopted a victim or 'poor me' attitude, you disempower yourself from living an authentically happy life. It is time to face and embrace past hurts and hang ups; forgive any wrongdoers – including yourself, process them and bid them adieu. What happened ten years ago or even ten minutes ago is done. You have a choice to bury negative emotions or embrace them, process them, and let them go. I understand that it is not easy and it is certainly a process which requires time, patience and courage. I know of a woman who hid her pain for over twenty years until her life had become so unmanageable she had a mental breakdown. She could not hide it no longer and an avalanche of negative emotions and pain flooded her being. She did not know what hit her. She could not figure out why she was so emotional because she'd always been so strong and in control.

What happened equated to a balloon that gets filled up with too much air, which eventually pops – her spirit absorbed all the pain and negative emotions it could take until it "popped." Her life was miserable for a long time thereafter as she sought refuge with various mental health professionals in an attempt to heal the pain. Fortunately, she came across someone who knew what she was dealing with and pointed her to a good therapist and support group. She worked through her pain and allowed past wounds to heal. She took responsibility for her emotional life and reclaimed her power. She courageously faced her painful past, did a lot of journaling and started a new journey toward wholeness. She now looks forward to her future while enjoying her present. Her emotional breakdown she now calls a 'spiritual transformation'.

Have you faced the wounds of your past? Do you feel a gnawing deep in your soul that wants your attention but you keep it at bay? Do you stuff your painful feelings away? Do you feel like a victim, unable to truly love yourself? Unworthy? Angry? Bitter? It is in dealing with the past that you begin to create a prosperous and inviting future to look forward to. Carrying painful memories with you is a battle that you are less likely to win in the long run. When an emotion or group of emotions have sought their moment to be expressed, a wall of painful memories may invite themselves through your body. Health professionals are now attributing many physiological conditions to repressed emotions. The branch of medicine known as psychoneuroimmunology (PNI) seeks to understand the psychological processes connected with the nervous and immune systems of the human body.

It has been thought that the body carries the painful memory of the emotion in an attempt to move it through the system. Unfortunately it may get stuck in a body system, organ or muscle and remain dormant for many years until the individual has dealt with the toxic emotion. People often dismiss this area calling it New Age mumbo jumbo. The inference is based in the knowledge what you can't see won't hurt you. Yet I affirm that you cannot see or explain back pain, yet for many people the chronic and debilitating recurrence of this pain can be mentally, emotionally and physically taxing on the body if left unexamined. As you heal the past by dealing with the emotions in a healthy manner, you not only make peace with the disempowering emotions, you heal an aspect of your past self. This past self cannot create a remarkable and prosperous future if it continues to carry its pain and burden, all the while the emotional burden grows bigger each day until it can take no more and pops.

Face Your Demons

It is true that in order to make peace with the past, it is vital that you confront your demons. Facing your demons confronts the repressed or unconscious aspects of yourself in a healthy manner. You may have repressed the emotions for a variety of reasons, one of which is to prevent oneself from being hurt at the time. As we discussed earlier in the book, the mind defers the pain to a later period – although this later period never arrives and the emotions grow stronger with the passing of time. However, like an iceberg, 95 per cent of it remains submerged underwater; the unconscious mind is in many ways like the iceberg with mental processes obstructed from view. Your subconscious mind accounts for a great deal of your voluntary and involuntary actions. In the book *Subliminal*, author Leonard Mlodinow states the following about the function of the subconscious mind, *"Some scientist's estimate that we are conscious of only about 5 per cent of our cognitive function. The other 96 per cent goes on beyond our awareness and exerts a huge influence on our lives – beginning with making our lives possible."*

Through awareness and understanding, you become aware of your unconscious actions, so as not to become a victim to the programmed patterns which accompany them. These patterns consist of thoughts, ideas and behaviours we hold as absolute truth about our world. Unless questioned and examined, these thoughts remain dormant until they are called upon. Much like a computer whose keys are pressed, unconscious thoughts and behaviours leap into action without so much as being questioned and therein lies the problem.

Everything you desire lies on the other side of your demons. Your demons represent your fears, insecurities, doubts or negative beliefs and may become the source of suffering if left unexamined. To create a remarkable life, it is imperative to break through the glass ceiling obscured by your demons by making peace with the past and thus integrating your demons into the wholeness of your being. The shadow self is an aspect of oneself, which we deny or hide. It is a part of our unconscious mind consisting of one's repressed weaknesses and shortcomings. Carl Jung, the famous Swiss psychologist, said that the shadow creates a fog of illusion that surrounds the self. We become trapped in this fog and so transfer power to the shadow self. Much has been written about defeating and overcoming the shadow, while in essence we must learn to embrace it and integrate it, rather than disown it. For in doing so we seek to understand our true nature is merely but the union of light and dark.

Undertaking the process of self-examination assumes there are no guarantees of integrating into the wholeness of your being – yet it is certainly a step in the right direction and will offer many positive outcomes along the way. However, to attain your goals confronting your demons becomes paramount since the future cannot be realised by carrying the weight of your baggage from the past. Do not allow the past to be drawn into the future, unless you make peace with it. As you follow your path, the past may come back to revisit you in a number of ways. It does so to remind you of the neglected aspects that become essential to aid your personal growth. If you unconsciously ignored dealing with a powerful belief or emotion at the time, it lays dormant at the unconscious level without your awareness. Similarly it serves to remind you of unfinished business, which requires your attention. You may never know when your demons may surface; yet they may resurface at an inopportune time in your life when you are emotionally vulnerable.

If there is an aspect of your life which is the cause of unhappiness, attend to it by making peace with it. Discover what the belief or emotion wants you to understand by examining it with an open mind and self-directed compassion. Having undertaken the process years ago, I became aware of powerful emotions which I believed I had attended to many years earlier. Unknowingly, they remerged when other related complications in my life surfaced. Instead of shoving the emotion back down, I sought to address them in order to uncover the lesson contained within. As I attended to the disempowering emotional states by feeling them at a deeper level, they revealed an encouraging aspect of my personality, which I failed to recognise at the time. Your demons change form when you face them. They transform into a gateway toward joy and bliss. Whilst repressed emotions may appear as a negative state as a result of being suppressed, allowing them expression through you closes the gateway between the past and the future. This allows you to transition from the past into the future without having the weight of the past to bring along.

Consider a friend who calls you often yet you never bother to return their call. In due course the friend gets angry since they are at a loss to understand what they have done wrong and why you have not returned their call. While this analogy may be a simple representation of what transpires at a deeper emotional level, it nonetheless highlights how your beliefs and emotions have the power to transform energy into destructive ones if left unchecked. You may wish to think of it as the angry friend who in trying to make sense of why you have not bothered to return their calls, enacts revenge on you when you least expect it. As you attend to the emotion, it naturally reveals vital lessons, which are essential to your personal development whilst simultaneously healing the past by closing the wound on the pain which has taken place.

The important aspect of self-examination is the *willingness* to address the repressed emotions or beliefs. Without the desire to *clean out the closet* so to speak, you remain victim to the emotion. It haunts you until it grows larger and more powerful in magnitude. Give yourself permission to deal with the source of your unhappiness. Even if you do not know how; it is certainly better than living in fear of life collapsing beneath you. I have witnessed people overcome with such an intensity of buried emotions, it ruined their life. They fell victim to the ensuing emotions that eventually overpowered them. You will know when you are ready to examine your buried emotions. Your readiness will be heralded to face the past with compassion rather than regret or guilt. These too are toxic emotions which should not be referenced as you heal the past. Do not allow any negative or untoward feelings that are not essential to your emotional healing come between you and the remarkable future which awaits you. While it may seem frightening at first to deal with negative emotional states, it pails into insignificance to the havoc wreaked if the emotions are left unchecked. Be kind and patient with yourself during this process. You will experience a spectrum of emotions that bring you closer toward unveiling your authentic self.

Allow your light to shine on your demons. Like walking into a dark room to turn on the light which overpowers the darkness. Allowing your light to shine on your demons signifies the essence and spirit of your true nature. Through your spiritual work you discover there is more to you than a body and a mind. You discover that you are a boundless being with unlimited potential. Your potential becomes apparent when your demons are no longer the source of your pain. Like a prisoner held captive, your demons have the potential to generate the same effect if you do not make peace with them. Allowing your light to shine on your demons invites you to go within to discover the source of the energy. During meditation I am reminded of this energy as a flickering white light that I see and feel. As I connect and embrace this light, I realise the perfection and loving nature of my spirit calling me forth into the world. It is reassuring and inviting – it asks nothing of me other than I connect with it in an open and loving manner. For in connecting with it, I become the source of pure love and light. I recognise this quality as it *feels familiar*. It is kind, patient and non-judgemental. It does not ask anything of me – yet I am drawn to it.

You have this source of energy within you. By going into regular silence through meditation or being alone in nature, you will become familiar with it. As you unite with this expansive energy, others become aware of your light and cannot help to be drawn to you like a moth to a flame – you light the way for others to reveal their authentic self. Face your demons by seeking to liberate yourself from an imprisoned past. Ask for guidance from those you trust if you are unsure where to begin. Invite loved ones to help you realise aspects of yourself you wish to work through. Be gentle on yourself as you undertake this process. Do not pass judgement or criticism on *what is* – merely observe through silent awareness. In doing so you not only liberate yourself from that past, you create a porthole into an unlimited future.

Practicing Self-Compassion and Self-Acceptance

As you make peace with the past there are two essential components one must face as part of the healing process. Self-acceptance and self-compassion are two vital ingredients which must be sown into the fabric of the healing process in order to transcend past hurt and suffering. Earlier in the book I cited the work of Brené Brown who reminds us that owning our story is one of the most powerful and courageous steps one can take. There is great wisdom in accepting that we need not run away from who we are, rather we should face up to and own our story. This act alone opens the doorway to the healing process if we are to accept ourselves as we are. As you know pain and suffering abound when you go to war with yourself. This has been emphasised throughout the book as I believe it to be a central theme worth reiterating.

Similarly, self-compassion creates a comfortable and reassuring sanctuary for the healing process to take place. You treat yourself in a kind and compassionate manner by consoling yourself though the healing process. As you open old wounds to heal there may be a tendency to view them with scorn and criticism believing you acted in an untoward manner at the time. Hindsight is a wonderful thing and it is only when looking back on the past that we are able to see the error of our ways. We do so since we have attained perspective and a measure upon which to measure the past against. In her book *Radical Acceptance*, author and spiritual Buddhist teacher Tara Brach offers the following words of the importance of self-compassion in healing our heart from the pain of the past, *"Whenever we've become addicted to judging and mistrusting ourselves, any sincere gesture of care to the wounded places can bring about radical transformation. Our suffering then becomes a gateway to the compassion that can free our heart."*

Have you noticed some people just seem to be happy and content in their own skin most of the time? Do you know people who are miserable and pessimistic day in and day out? How about you? What are your predominant feelings toward life? From the time we are children, it seems that many have lived a life of some sort of emotional abandonment, leaving them living a life with their mental script less than optimal and often quite negative. They are hard on themselves and that harshness tends to affect every area of their lives. Emotional abandonment means one tends to run from fulfilling emotional needs instead of embracing that they need self-love and self-acceptance. Even young children can begin to think the thoughts, "I don't like myself" and "I'm not worthy" and unfortunately, carry those thoughts throughout their lives.

Maybe all of your emotional needs were not met as a child and as a result, you grew up with low self-esteem and low self-worth. This is a common scenario in our society. For one reason or another, babies and children begin their lives believing they are not worth much. They go through life stuffing the pain associated with such and/or try to cover up that pain with addictions, people, success, or material possessions. This poses a huge problem because going through life like this makes for a miserable existence and leads to things like depression, severe anxiety, mental health disorders, and tremendous pain. The good news is that plenty of people have faced their inner struggles with low self-worth and lack of self-compassion and have learned how to love themselves wholeheartedly. They have become vulnerable and faced their insecurities, disappointments, pain, and so much more in order to learn the art of self-compassion and acceptance. In fact, part of an adult's life journey oftentimes leads them in a direction where they will have to face the darkness in order to walk more fully in the light. Sometimes growth requires walking through pain in order to find oneself among the broken ruins.

Everyone encounters some pain on their life journey. It begins in childhood and continues throughout life. What people do with inner wounds that come from pain will determine their attitude and actions throughout life. Inner wounds lead people to persecute themselves. They think "I must deserve this" or "I'll never be good enough". That type of thinking tends to keep them in a state of unworthiness. The truth is that people tend to be so hard on themselves and they do not realise that they can learn to adore who they are despite their pasts and their pain. Learning self-love and self-compassion is possible and it begins with coming to that understanding that you do matter. You are worthy in and of yourself. You can love yourself and treat yourself with compassion. It is wonderful to treat others with compassion, but do you treat yourself that way? Do you delight in yourself? Believe in yourself?

Begin with looking in the mirror and see yourself as beautiful and worthy. Declare that you are worthy of love and anything that may have taken place in the past has only served your personal growth. Accept you for who you are: *your flaws are your assets*. Embody these aspects rather than disown them or run away from them. No one is perfect and you are no exception. Seeking perfection is a futile battle bound to cause more anxiety and frustration – strive for excellence instead. Embrace all of you exactly as you are. There is no need to change anything or fix anything for you are not broken – abandon this way of thinking in favour of embracing your wholeness. You will notice as you connect with your wholeness, others will mirror this aspect of yourself in their interaction with you. Life will make sense because you will be in tune with your authentic self, which is at the core – LOVE.

Transforming Guilt and Shame

As you embark on your journey towards making peace with your past, there are two emotional states which carry a stronger burden – guilt and shame. Healing these two states not only liberates you from carrying the burden of the past into the present moment, but the accompanying emotions of fear and anxiety are subsequently healed. Fear and anxiety accompany guilt and shame since there is an underlying fear connected to feelings of guilt. The shameful person fears being found out or exposed for their deep feelings towards oneself, although this tends to be an invalid thought process. Guilt is defined as a deep feeling of remorse for an act which may or may not have occurred in the past. Therefore, guilt becomes a past experience which is renewed in the present moment. We continue to replay the emotional state associated with guilt believing we are unworthy of making peace with the past. Guilt and the conscious are synonymously tied. It is a misperception that there is a right or wrong course of action, and subsequently the person ties a connection to having performed a wrongful act in the past for which they should be punished for. They continue to perpetuate the scolded inner child since they feel unworthy of attaining inner peace. There is a misguided thinking which imposes the thought, *"Since I committed an untoward act, I deserved to be punished and carry the guilt with me."*

However, showing mercy towards oneself can be the greatest act of kindness and healing process to release the burden of the past. Showing mercy towards oneself liberates you from no longer carrying the guilt into the future. You were doing the best you could at the time given the resources apparent to you. As we journey through life and acquire a better understanding and awareness, typically we look back on the past with a feeling of regret and remorse for our actions. What if in looking back on your past you did so with a compassionate heart filled with forgiveness rather than guilt? Release the burden of carrying the guilt into the present moment for in doing so you not only heal the past, you simultaneously bring new life to the present and future.

In a similar vein, shame is viewed as a product of failing to live up to an imagined ideal of oneself. We create an image of who we should be from a young age, which is the accumulation of the thoughts and ideals of those whom we love and respect. Unfortunately for a number of people, these ideals may no longer serve them as they undertake a new life path or embark upon a spiritual journey of self-discovery. Shame may also be reflected in the ideals held by society. Popular culture affirms a set of principles and conduct one must conform to if they are to be deemed worthy within the context of the tribe. There are a set of do's and don'ts which are typically acquired in adolescence and this is no more evident within the context of marriage. Marriage and family are viewed as natural developments into adulthood for the young male and female. Do not get divorced. Do not cheat on your husband/wife. Whilst there is some merit in being a virtuous citizen, upholding morale places restrictions that do not serve those who fall out of the bounds of these obligations.

Shame creates an unrealistic measure of self-worth, since you create a point of separation between who you think you should be who and you who actually are. This creates the basis for shame since you feel unworthy of measuring up to the image perpetuated in the mind. It must be said that this is merely a mirage – a canvas created by the mind in which you attempt to live up to. Yet if you fail to live up to this image of oneself, suffering ensues since there is a divide between the imagined self and the proposed self. The accumulation of shame can lead to depression and anxiety, notwithstanding the image of being shamed. For many people living this way may be considered normal, since they have no contrasting reference points advising them on how they should really feel.

We internalise shame since we feel it is inappropriate to be angry, sad, depressed or otherwise. We endeavour to uphold an image that society has depicted of a well-adjusted and happy individual who is devoid of toxic emotions. After all, who wants to know a dysfunctional individual who is incapable of handling their emotional state in a healthy manner? This is the message which many people unwittingly buy into, believing they need to suppress or mask their emotions in order to appear 'normal.' Yet masking one's true emotions to appear normal does little to hide the truth, when your emotions rupture and overwhelm you – by then it is too late. Successively, many people are ashamed to express their emotions for fear they will be judged – in some cultures, such as the Japanese, suppressing their emotions is considered normal in comparison to their European neighbours who are open in their emotional expression.

Therefore, to move through shame we must be willing to become aware of our internal emotional state. That is to recognise that we are living with shame, rather than deny or suppress the emotion. Awareness opens the gateway to the next healing doorway. There must be willingness to accept our internal state rather than oppose it – embrace the shame rather than running away from it or disown it. *"I have the feeling of shame"* becomes a healthier inner affirmation rather than, *"I am ashamed for my past actions."* Finally, expressing oneself is the final doorway to the healing process, since one needs to share and explore their feelings with others or a trained therapist in order to connect with their emotions at a deeper level and subsequently transform them into empowering ones. There is a spiritual message contained within the experience of shame. Namely, shame obscures the real and authentic self waiting to emerge from behind the veil of pride.

Learning to Love Yourself Again

Just as it is important to transform guilt and shame into positive emotional states, it is equally important for the individual to learn to love him/herself again. When you do not love yourself, it is hard to expect others to love you. Agreed, we may have many faults and shortcomings. There must be a willingness to embrace yourself with all your faults by learning to love yourself again. Self-love and self-esteem are inextricably related to each other. If you suffer low esteem, there is inadequate self-love. With low confidence, you find it difficult to love yourself at first, since you do not think highly of yourself. Low confidence may be an internal script perpetuated in childhood where a parent or loved one inappropriately judged you as living up to their expectations. As you learn to love yourself again, your self-esteem is subsequently enhanced, resulting in higher self-confidence. Loving yourself must be met through conscious will. It is a decision you must be willing to reach in order to live a remarkable future. By entertaining low self-esteem, one is unable to reach their full potential. It is similar to the story of baby circus elephants who are tethered to a chain and post in the ground at a young age. As they mature to full adults, they have acquired the mental conditioning of being tied to the chain, irrespective of their size and force to break free.

Consider the following points as you embark on a journey of self-love. There may be a tendency to invite the inner critic to rear its ugly head as you take the path of self-love. Remember, do not believe everything you think. Thoughts have no effect on the authentic self who is connected with the light of their being, rather than the false perception of self.

Understand yourself: You must endeavour to understand yourself at a deeper level and know what makes you bloom. I am not advocating that you know your dislikes or likes since this is superficial and changes with time. You may have many flaws, but you must accept them and move on. There is no prize awarded to the person who wallows in self-pity or self-deprecation. Here is the mail - nobody is perfect. Yes, even the most perfect person you have met or idolise has flaws. You are not the only one. Stand in front of a mirror and admire your reflection while falling in love with yourself. I have witnessed countless individuals perform this act and break down in tears at the very thought of directing love towards themselves. They are immediately overwhelmed with a feeling of unworthiness. Who ever said so? You might not be as important for others, but in your life story, you are the hero, and your life revolves around you.

Avoid self-criticism: Do you often demean yourself over small things? Whenever you make any small mistake, are you aware of a voice inside your head telling you that you are inadequate and unworthy? Self-criticism may be a learned response from early childhood. This is no more evident than with elite athletes who are self-critical when their performance suffers. Did you know that by the time you reach adulthood, you would have heard the word 'NO' repeated 50,000 times throughout your life? In contrast the word 'YES' is only heard 7,000 times. It is no wonder self-criticism manages to weave its way into our minds with such intensity. We are notorious for falsifying inaccurate tales about ourselves. Self-criticism is one such story often repeated through adulthood. Whilst it is healthy to be mildly critical of one's performance from time to time, being at the mercy of the debilitating thought is not conducive toward living a fulfilling life. In a similar vein, self-criticism can become self-deprecating while wreaking havoc with your personal confidence if left unchecked. Take measures to become attuned to the inner dialogue or inner critic which resides within. Take appropriate action to rewrite a more prominent internal script, rather than be at the mercy of harmful thoughts.

The power of empowering thoughts: As you embrace empowering thoughts, you become kinder towards yourself and your self-love increases. Negative thinking is like wearing dirty and dark glasses, because it fogs our vision and gives a highly distorted image of reality. When you entertain negative thoughts, you cannot find joy in life as your entire mindset convinces you that joy and happiness are not an option for you, and even if you are feeling some happiness, it is only temporary. Negative thinking leads to negative actions, which creates a wall between you and others. No matter how kind and open others may be, you will not be able to trust them if you do not have a positive outlook towards life. Your negativity will lead you into thinking their kindness is not genuine. Your perception of reality is obscured by murky thoughts. Negative thinking patterns are not naturally acquired- they are learned. When we get the light of positivity, we can see negativity clearly without giving ourselves a bad time mulling over it. This is when we decide to change ourselves and our way of thinking. It lightens up the heavy burden on our personality.

Overcome obstacles: Obstacles are present in everyday life, be it a barrier that sets you back, halts your progress or derails your best laid plans. They can be discouraging and cause loss of precious time and resources. Beyond the cause of frustration what purpose do obstacles serve? Could there be a gift contained within the experience? Perhaps you need to become acquainted with a certain skill or acquire valuable knowledge before proceeding with your plans. We must consider that obstacles serve a function other than causing emotional distress. Contesting reality will not earn you support, since life always prevails. Leaning in to your challenges however, allows you to move THROUGH the obstacle rather than allow it to dominate your life. By leaning in to your challenges, you welcome the flow of life through your non-resistance. You allow the obstacle to permeate your life in order to identify the significance of the hurdle. Be willing to abandon endeavours that do not deliver results. Far too many people discount the value of redirecting their attention elsewhere when all attempts have been exhausted. Pride, self-worth and time invested are the main reasons cited for flogging a dead horse.

Release expectations: Expectations limit the flow of life's experiences by the layers we add to rationalise the world, albeit at a cost of limiting our perspective.

As we gain trust in the rhythm of life, we acquire confidence through our attentiveness to the signs life bestows us. Firstly, experience the world through the eyes of a child. Surrender all expectations as you remain fascinated by uncertainty and ambiguity, which are the birthplaces of creation. Secondly, stay grounded and present – this allows you to let go of future expectations and the need to recycle the past in to the present moment. Remaining present invites you to embody life's experiences with fullness. Remember Krishna Sagaar's advice, *"You don't see the world as it is, you see it, as you are."* Thus we do not experience reality as we believe, but through a self-made filter of our accumulated beliefs, thoughts and emotions carried with us over time. In addition, seek to get out of your head and into your heart. Abandon your fantasies about what life owes you. Life does not serve to fulfil your every request like an online order catalogue. The moment you engage life with purpose and passion, your expectations will no longer dominate your thought landscape – all your needs will arrive precisely at the right time, when you least expect them.

Forgive yourself: We all make mistakes. No doubt you have also made some mistakes throughout your life. If you are holding on to your mistakes and playing them out in your mind, you are moving away from creating a powerful future. Learn to forgive yourself by reframing the mistakes as a learning curve. If you stay trapped in a process of recycling the past, your reference point becomes the past and not the present moment. It is fine to concede mistakes were made and forgiveness is a process of shining a light on those mistakes by bringing compassion to the situation. People go to church to be absolved of their sins, and similarly, Christianity teaches that God forgives us all for our transgressions. You need not carry the cross of the past any longer. Forgive yourself – forgive those who co-created any untoward experience at the same time. It need not happen overnight, allow the process to unfold, although it is vital to have a wilful intent to embrace forgiveness as a healing process toward living a promising future. Believe in yourself and know that whatever was done in the past was not intentional. The decisions and actions taken were done so with what you knew best at the time. As you learned and gained more insight with the passing of time, you were able to make more empowering life choices which corresponded with your outlook on life. In a similar vein, know that you have learned a lesson and that your mistakes will not be repeated again.

Spiritual truth: Being spiritually aligned means discovering the essence of your being and the deepest values by which you live. You connect to a higher source of intelligence or power, identifying with something greater than the material world. Being spiritual becomes a way of life. People often embark on a spiritual path, devoting time to principles that bring them closer to their source.

Prayer, meditation, yoga and self-awareness are a few practices undertaken to connect to infinite intelligence. When you are spiritually aligned, you connect to the source of an intelligence, which guides and creates the universe, including ourselves. In the book *Soul Medicine* by Dr. Dawson Church and Larry Dossey, the author's state, *"That paying attention to your spiritual life is the most important thing you can do for your health."* They identify twelve characteristics common to people with a vibrant soul connection; these include:

Forgiveness	Motivation
Tolerance	Consistency
Serenity	Community
Faith	Joy
Reason	Gratitude
Hope	Love

Aligning with spiritual truth means developing a profound belief – an inner knowing outside of the material realm we have come to know and trust. One begins to develop and be guided by other faculties such as; intuition and synchronicities. We are not beings limited to our five senses. Meditation allows you to understand and commune with the deeper self, to know the essence of your spirit. You discover purpose and meaning to your life via self-discovery. In order to live an enriching life imbued with health and happiness you must connect to that source, which nourishes you. Spirituality allows you to develop a deeper understanding of your role in this purposeful universe. You are at peace within yourself. In doing so, you surrender striving – instead the more you let go of, the more flows into your life.

Develop an attitude of gratitude: Being grateful does not mean comparing oneself to others who are less fortunate; for we all have our own journey in life. Mahatma Gandhi said this so eloquently – *"Be the change you want to see in the world."* Start with simple things to be grateful for and watch your energy rise. You begin attracting circumstances in to your life as though each event was a miracle. People, places, things begin showing up almost instantly to remind you that your energy level is expanding in the right direction. Life reminds us in no uncertain terms, how grateful we are when we see others doing it tough or when we are going through our own hardship. There is light at the end of the tunnel, for as sure as the season's change, so too will your circumstances when you begin to live in congruency with your highest self. Begin your journey of gratitude with the smallest gestures – a simple thank *you to the universe as you retire to bed each night is a good starting point. Often when I lay my head down to rest at night, I think about the homeless person my age, sleeping outside in the cold somewhere. That thought alone ignites a deep, powerful sense of thankfulness for having a comfortable, warm bed to sleep in – I feel safe and a renewed trust that I am loved and cared for.*

CHAPTER 6

Lessons on Forgiveness

Forgive and Release the Past

*"Forgiving does not erase the bitter past. A healed memory is not a deleted memory.
Instead, forgiving what we cannot forget creates a new way to remember. We change
the memory of our past into a hope for our future."* — Louis B. Smedes

Your emotional connection to the past is vital to your perception of life. To forgive
the past is paramount to creating a remarkable future worth looking forward to.
Many people experience life trapped and haunted by their emotional links to
the past as we have outlined in previous chapters. They continue to recycle
past memories into the present moment, which deprives them of enjoying the
fullness of the now experience. Allow me, to highlight an example using myself.
My connection to the notion of self-love evaded me at a deeper level. While
I understood it at an intellectual level; at a soul level I found it challenging to
embrace. Upon closer self-examination, I realised the source of my emotional
disconnect was an inaccurate belief formed when young.

How do you know? Look closely at the aspects of your life which cause you
distress. Are they relationships woes? Is it money related; health, career or other?
You may be aware of the same patterns for a number of years while powerless to
navigate your way out of it. Limited beliefs have their source at the unconscious
level of the mind. You are subject to repeating the same mistake until the belief
is brought to the forefront of your mind and made conscious. In hindsight, you
see very little explanation as to why you behaved that way.

Unconscious thought patterns.

Listed below are a number of examples how limited beliefs may show up in your life:

1. You unconsciously spend money you do not have and wonder why you
   struggle with your finances.

2. You repeatedly attract the wrong type of romantic partner.
3. You sabotage your relationships when things are moving in the right direction.
4. You miss out on job promotions even though you work just as hard as the person who gets them.
5. You gravitate toward unhealthy food options after you have started a new health regime.

The above points are indicators you may be holding an unconscious belief related to that area of life. In clarifying those points, here are my recommendations in the particular order as to what the unconscious belief may reveal.

1. Unconscious belief: receiving, self-esteem or unworthiness.
2. Unconscious belief: low self-esteem, unworthiness or fear.
3. Unconscious belief: fear, change, fear of the past or success.
4. Unconscious belief: fear of success, self-esteem, unworthiness.
5. Unconscious belief: fear of failure, self-esteem, unworthiness.

The key is knowing which belief to work through to release the past memories and hurts that haunt you in the present moment. A good analogy for clearing the past would look like this. Consider a person who frequently refers to their past successes and failures. They might use words like, *"I used to be..."* or *"I used to do..."* What they are telling you is that *"I am an amalgamation of my past success and/or failures - I choose to relive them in this present moment."* They are defined by their past mistakes or success while not engaged in the present moment. The present moment is your key to the future. Your memories are purely a figment of your imagination. I am not suggesting you deny your memories; rather that you refrain from habitually referencing them in order to define yourself NOW, that is, unless the memory is success related. Make a vow to forgive and release the past in order to live a deep and meaningful life. Refuse to be a victim to your thoughts and emotions. You will know you are making progress when you see those unconscious habits fall away, thus experiencing your heart's desires. Create a space in your heart for that which you seek and fill it with love. Whatever you look for awaits you on the other side of your fears and doubts - so claim them now.

The Unexamined Life

Many of us sail through life impervious to the choices we make each day. Such decisions are often made without even second guessing ourselves. We discover that many of these choices are programmed, that is they are devoid of conscious intent. As time goes by we pause and reflect how such choices were made, realising that we have not been as present after all. Socrates, the Greek philosopher and founder of Western Philosophy coined the phrase, *"The unexamined life is not worth living"* circa 470 – 399 BC. There have been countless explorations of this passage over time, yet he was referring to our capacity to attain self-mastery via self-examination at our deepest essence. We can live a virtuous life through regular self-examination, which opens a pathway toward forgiveness. Knowing ourselves at the deeper level allows forgiveness to permeate through our lives, while realising that everything is perfect as it should be. There is no need to oppose the forces of life when we undertake this understanding, as long as we are heading down the right spiritual path.

Self-awareness is one of the key attributes humans possess, which distinguishes us from the animal kingdom. The notable mirror test developed by the psychologist Gordon Gallup Jnr. is used an indicator of awareness in animals. In this experiment, animals are presented with an image of themselves reflected back via a mirror. If they recognise the image reflected back (often a marking is made on the animal to determine if they identify it), then it is deemed that they are self-aware. Interestingly, children tend to fail this test until they are at least 1.5 to 2 years old. Therefore, self-awareness is the bedrock upon which we identify with our being. It allows us to interact with others and our environment through our experience of the world. Being self-aware not only attributes an awareness of self, it signifies an understanding of one's personality, i.e. strengths, weaknesses, thoughts, beliefs and motivation. In contrast, there are many people who sail through life oblivious to their behaviour. They rarely learn from their mistakes, since they are programmed from early childhood to disregard the impact of their actions. It might be said that their self-awareness is limited. Such people are unaware of the mental and emotional prejudices accrued over time. It has been said that we spend the first half of our life accumulating knowledge and the second half letting go of that knowledge.

Devoid of our capacity for self-examination, it may seem as though life is acting upon us as we fall victim to the forces of life. Alternatively, as we let go of the distorted thinking, we appreciate that as agents of free choice acting within the container of free will, we are indeed co-creating our life's circumstances. It posits favourably that since we have free will, we should strive to make decisions that are in line with our best interests. Our aim should be to uphold the essential virtues of human existence: wisdom, justice, forgiveness, self-control, love, a positive attitude, hard work, integrity, gratitude and humility. Authenticity describes the act of living in congruency with our highest nature. Rather than abide by our external environment, we become blissfully aware of our inner nature as we strive to uphold the human virtues.

Self-examination in this context becomes an expression of knowing oneself. Fundamentally, our aim at this level is to overcome our mistakes and grant forgiveness towards ourselves and others. In doing so we refuse to invite those same mistakes into the future and thus heal the past. Two vital ingredients are required for self-mastery: **personal growth** and **self-awareness**. Much like brushing our teeth to keep them clean, attending to our personal growth on a daily basis is like exercise for our mental wellbeing. Moreover, self-awareness coupled with personal growth may be akin to a gardener pulling weeds while simultaneously harvesting a new crop. In time, not only have we cultivated an entire garden devoid of weeds, we have simultaneously allowed our authentic self to emerge.

In my previous book, *The Power to Navigate Life*, I invited the reader to consider two ideas dutifully essential to self-mastery. I affirmed that you are either *Navigating Life* or *Parked*. A *Parked* state may be characterised by the metaphysical relationship one experiences while in a motor vehicle when stationary: stopped, stuck, enclosed, stagnant, not moving and trapped. *Navigating Life* on the other hand denotes a movement of outward energy: expansive, moving freely, navigating, exploring, discovering and expressive. These two states represent the metaphysical relationship we have with ourselves at certain times of our life. As we learn to reclaim our internal state, we move from a *Parked* state to *Navigating Life*. It must be said that even while you may be *Parked*, it serves as a valuable opportunity for self-reflection so you do not carry those mistakes into the future. Your aim is to move forward in life while not bringing the baggage of the past along. Baggage carried over time can become heavy and overflow. Forgiveness is the valve which allows the injured past to be slowly released and transformed so as to create a compelling future. A deep and meaningful life is worth living if we become self-aware and strive to lead an authentic life. Through regular self-examination we appreciate that there are no right or wrong actions, only consequences. In order to reduce the likelihood of experiencing untoward outcomes, we connect with our deepest self, which is the essence of our authentic nature.

Stop Punishing Yourself

Self-punishment may be the single biggest aspect holding you back from living an empowered life if it is not attended to with kindness and self-compassion. Self-punishment may be a learned response from parents or loved ones when you were a child. The critical parent can sometimes be disparaging in their words while not realising the gravity that such words have on the subconscious programming of the child. I was brought up in a very loving and nurturing home environment, yet I was subject to parental discipline by a father whose standards I could not live up to. It seemed that nothing I did was ever good enough – according to my father there was always an opportunity to improve. Although to a young boy looking up to his father, reassurance and emotional support are required to nurture a child's development. It was in my adult years, which I recounted earlier, that I unconsciously adopted much of the same behaviour towards myself. I was acting out the behaviour I was all too familiar with as a child. It was not until I took some time to reflect and examine my behaviours that I came to realise I was enacting my father's behaviour towards me as a child.

Self-punishment appears to be a defence mechanism intended to support the difficulties of life. Over the years I have heard countless stories of people describing in detail how difficult and unjust life can be. Being emotionally resilient allows a person to withstand the forces of life. Yet, this is not how it is supposed to be. Emotionally resilience does not call for self-punishment in order to become emotionally stronger. In fact, as you know, it has the opposite effect. One of the aspects I discovered in my self-reflection was the strong need as a young boy for my father to reinforce my good behaviour. I craved reassurance as a child and would supplicate to him in order to appeal to his good nature. In effect, I was seeking consolation and caring – to be nurtured so as to develop a healthy self-esteem. Therefore, emotional resiliency is borne out of a prominent self-worth. Your inner child craves to be nurtured in a loving and kind manner, much like you would treat a loved one.

If our emotional needs are not met, we develop disempowering emotions, such as anger and rage, which is turned on oneself. The self-punishing person suddenly develops a harsh inner critic and voice which advises him/her that nothing they do is good enough. You may have been in this situation yourself over the years? Such dialogue as, *"You idiot! Why do I keep making these stupid mistakes? I am such a fool"* only reinforce the self-punishment at a subconscious level. As you pose disempowering questions, the mind becomes habituated towards providing the answers to these questions and soon enough a cycle of self-deprecation ensues. At this stage, the individual has adopted the persona of the inner critic as part of their personality where it has become a part of who they believe themselves to be.

The key to working through self-punishment is to recognise that our thoughts are deeply ingrained having been reinforced over many years. It will require a concerted effort and patience to move through this phase of reconciliation. Changing your inner dialogue to be pleasant overnight may be seen as a threat to the ego, since you have become accustomed to the voice of the inner critic.

Positive self-talk in this instance may be akin to speaking in another tongue. Whilst the nature of the self-directed inner talk may be familiar, it does not feel true since you have grown accustomed to the self-punishing talk over time. In a previous chapter I outlined how guilt imposes itself in such a way to appease ourselves for wrongful actions. We unconsciously punish ourselves since this is viewed as self-retribution for untoward action in the past. People at this level who typically feel bad about themselves will develop a harsh inner critic who feels compelled to punish oneself for wrongful acts.

We previously examined the role of forgiveness in previous chapters as a means to rewrite the past and invite love and compassionate energy towards oneself. If we are to be realistic, this may pose more challenges than we anticipate, given that we are attempting to rewrite a strong and powerful inner script that has been given power all these years. I affirm that as we attend to our shame and guilt, we become less critical of ourselves and slowly turn down the volume on the self-punishing inner critic. The answer lies in transforming the self-punishing inner talk, rather than obliterate it completely. The transformation process seeks to understand that we create a false sense of self by feeding this false-self power over us – yet this is not who we really are. Transforming self-punishment becomes an act of forgiveness and self-compassion by creating a new inner dialogue, which naturally unfolds over time. Working with a trained mental health professional is advised as a means to begin the process of healing, while simultaneously developing a new vista upon which to heal one's past.

At times there may be a great deal of pain that has accumulated over the years that seems unbearable to deal with, so we delay the healing process. We must come to terms with feeling the pain within the context of a secure and nurturing setting if we are to move forward and transform the self-punishment into positive energy. As you develop a nurturing inner self, this feeling naturally polarises over time to create a new lens in which to view our past wounds. Therefore, we realise that we are capable of managing real-life problems by our capacity to develop a stronger emotional resilience, which is not vested in self-deprecating inner talk.

Don't Believe Everything You Think

I invite you to consider the role your thoughts have in cultivating forgiveness towards your past. Thoughts seem to arise out of nowhere and wreak havoc when we buy into the false message they offer. The Buddhist principle states; you are not the sum of your thoughts, rather the observer of the thoughts. A number of people regularly entertain limiting thoughts, which are grounded in an inaccurate reality - *"I am not good enough," or "I am overweight."* Such thoughts lead to self-disparaging thoughts, which fuel the emotional body. The truth is your habitual thoughts do not represent the *real* you. Become an observer of your thoughts in much the same way as you would observe the scenery while riding the bus to work. As you become the observer of the thought, the question is posed, who is thinking the thought? Dissociating with your thoughts allows you to be removed from the habitual pattern of believing what you think. We believe a thought to be true since our experience of the thought leads us to confirm it must be factual. Opening the doorway to forgiveness means letting go of the unnecessary thoughts related to your past by recognising that thoughts are transient and do not define the person.

Managing unwanted thoughts proposes that you become a silent witness standing at the shoreline observing your thoughts as waves coming in. Some waves appear fast and furious, yet recede as they hit the shoreline. Others slowly make their way in to disappear with the same intensity. As the observer, you allow the witnessing of the thoughts to take shape by remaining detached from the stream of thoughts. The witness or observer does not become invested in the waves any more than respecting there will always be thoughts (waves) appearing in the mind. You become the seer of your thought process and cease to identify with them. In a similar vein, it has been estimated we entertain anywhere between 70,000 – 80,000 thoughts a day. Much of those thoughts are repetitive in nature. That is we rethink the same thoughts day in day out without much consideration. Recall the last time your thoughts were "stuck" as it were. No matter how hard you tried, the thoughts kept emerging – often in a fast and furious manner.

It must be appreciated that thoughts are simply thoughts. They come and go without an agenda. It is when we attach meaning to those thoughts that substance is created. Therefore, believing you are unworthy of forgiveness is an inaccurate thought supported by a false belief. Consider the same thought can have no impact at all at a point in time, yet other times it can cause mental and emotional distress, since we are continually responding and reacting to our external environment.

Regrettably, many people believe that because they regularly entertain thoughts, they must be true – that is not true, thoughts come and go all the time. There is no point attaching yourself to them since there is **no permanency** there. Thoughts only have the capacity to overwhelm us, since the meaning we assign to them fuels them with energy to thrive throughout our neural network. In due course when enough attention is given to a thought, it transforms into matter or may consequently affect your physiology. What does this mean? If I asked you to close your eyes and picture yourself eating your favourite ice-cream, you might recall a scene that involved tasting the ice-cream and engaging all the wonderful sensations that accompany it. Observing your thoughts is not dissimilar. As thoughts enter your mind, instead of communicating with them, simply observe them by becoming aware of their nature. You may wish to **label disempowering thoughts** as they emerge, so that your awareness becomes attuned to screening them. This means the next time they appear, your mind is adept at learning to recognise and filter un-useful thoughts.

For example; if visualising the ice-cream reminded you of an unpleasant experience, you might label the thought as sad or angry. They key is not to give life to the thought by dialoguing with it. Simply identify it and let it go. There are far too many thoughts running throughout your mind to catalogue them all. Overstimulation of thoughts may become a bad habit. Many busy people become addicted to incessant thoughts, i.e. *monkey mind* which denotes the difficulty to tame such thoughts. They feel empty without the mental drama, since that would mean being alone in silence. Consequently, this may bring up all manner of negative thoughts about one's self-worth. Consciousness knows and sees all. Next time you are at the park, observe the dogs or children playing. Your mind will naturally want to add a narrative to it, although your nervous system knows what it sees and feels. This is consciousness running in the background. You know a red kite when you see it, yet your mind feels drawn to add the thought "look at the bright red kite" to validate what it sees.

By simply turning down the narrative, you allow consciousness to observe your environment and reduce the stress on your mind and body. You need not identify with the thoughts that you are unworthy of forgiveness since you are buying into the falseness of that thought. From time to time observe your inner voice by becoming acquainted with the way it communicates to you. You have the power to master your thoughts related to your past by not becoming a slave to the internal chatter. As you become familiar with your inner domain, thoughts no longer have the capacity to control your life. You recognise the importance of forgiveness and the role it plays in balancing out past karma. You create a powerful lens in which to connect with the past and the future. You are no longer bound and imprisoned by self-defeating thoughts that remind you of your unworthiness.

CHAPTER 7

Let Go of the Pain

Stop Holding On To the Pain

"Renew, release, let go. Yesterday's gone. There's nothing you can do to bring it back. You can't "should've" done something. You can only DO something. Renew yourself. Release that attachment. Today is a new day!" — Steve Maraboli

Imagine life without the disorganised thoughts playing out inside your head. Imagine a state of peaceful thoughts, which come and go like the ocean tides – without struggle, pain or resistance. Are you holding on to any painful memories which you find difficult to let go of? Many people remain unconscious to these memories until they overwhelm them. Each time a painful memory is recalled, it is brought to life by inviting the past into the present. Have you experienced a moment throughout the day, when for no apparent reason you are drawn into a bad mood? Mood swings represent the unconscious-self recalling past memories. When we least expect them, negative emotions, such as anger, frustration, anxiety and sadness emerge. For some people holding onto pain signifies a badge of honour – it identifies them as one who has been victimised. They wear their badge to mark their identity and as a means to justify their victimisation.

In order to harness the richness of life, we must be willing to let go of our pain. We must drop the story that accompanies the pain. This begins with the desire to release the pain and suffering in order to allow the new, fresh and expansive energy of life to permeate through our being. By no means does this underscore the gravity of what occurred in the past. You choose not to carry the burden of the pain in the present moment and future. When we identify with our pain, we view the world through a distorted lens. Those fleeting moments of joy and happiness are lost to a mind that has spent years drawing on painful memories. You may have come across people who carry their victimisation with them. They use any opportunity to go to war with others when life does not play their tune. I see this frequently while shopping. Whilst standing in line I notice there may be only one checkout operator processing customer's purchases. The checkout operator grows distressed at the growing queue of people standing in line, yet is unable to go any faster. A person standing in queue quickly grows impatient for being made to wait more than necessary. They incite tension among other shoppers by rallying those who identified with their plight. This example is an all too common experience in everyday life. It illustrates how minor situations can derail us and cause mental and emotional unrest.

It takes a great deal of energy to keep the past alive. The mental and emotional resources required could be better spent on other rewarding life experiences. Over time, and if left untreated, painful memories have the capacity to transform into psychosomatic illnesses. Mental health professionals believe it takes approximately one and a half minutes for the body to process an emotion. Knowing this we need not hold onto mental and emotional pain from the past, nor do we need to carry it with us for years. Simply dealing with the emotion as it arises allows it to move through the body in a shorter amount of time and without the long term physiological effects. Often, people hold on to their pain for so long that it forms a safety blanket. They would feel lost without the pain and suffering. After all, they would have no story to tell. Perhaps others might find them uninteresting. Who would they be without their story?

Bad things happen to good people every day. They have happen to good people all throughout human history. One needs only look to the concentration camps in Nazi Germany during the war to see the devastation it had on the lives of so many innocent people. Despite the brutality, one man emerged in his personal statement against his aggressors. Viktor Frankl's quote highlights our power to transform external life's events into meaningful personal victories. He reminds us, *"Everything can be taken from a man but one thing: the last human freedoms – to choose one's attitude in any given set of circumstances, to choose one's own way."*

In order to release your pain, make an inner declaration to choose peace, happiness and freedom – even if you do not know how. Once you abide by this affirmation, the healing process has already begun and your unconscious mind will naturally move toward a state of peacefulness through your thoughts. You owe it to yourself and your loved ones to release yourself from the mental prison that has held you captive all this time. Life is far richer without the burden of painful memories. Victims never heal – they simply carry the wounded victim title around, showcasing it to people who will listen to their plight. It makes them feel acknowledged that they have suffered an indignity. Yet if you continue to feed and perpetuate this story, your mind naturally becomes accustomed to it by buying into it. That is why affirmations work – anything repeated often and with emotional intensity has the power to transform the subconscious mind and bring life to the thought.

In a previous chapter I outlined the case why you should not believe everything you think. The mind thrives on creating a storyline to substantiate what it sees or experiences. Yet awareness has the experience well before the mind has had time to create a thought to validate it. In his book *Simply Notice: Clear Awareness Is the Key To Happiness, Love and Freedom,* author Peter Francis Dziuban reinforces the idea of the mind seeking to add commentary to your life's experiences, *"Before something can clearly be seen or perceived for what it is, thinking is already adding judgements and commentary, acting like a smoke screen."* Therefore, if you constantly create a narrative around your emotional experiences, the mind creates a smoke screen, as the author suggests, to conceal what is really taking place beneath the surface. In time the real self becomes obscured by this screen since you have bought in to a false facade instead of the real story of your authenticity. To create a new and more empowering future requires that you create a space in your life to heal the past and subsequently release the pain. In order to release the pain you must be willing to engage the following attributes towards carving out a path towards inner peace and freedom.

Commitment: A person who has undergone mental and emotional trauma may find it difficult to let go of their suffering. As stated in a previous chapter, they protect themselves by erecting an emotional barrier which distances them from having to feel the emotions again or relive the mental anguish of the pain. Unfortunately the mind becomes astute at creating a barrier that in time becomes impenetrable to deal with the emotional wounds. Your commitment to healing the past by letting go of these wounds, is the first step in reconciling with the past. The commitment heralds the process of facing the past by bringing unresolved issues to the surface in order to heal them. The challenge posed with honouring this commitment arises when confronting the pain, since this can be overwhelming at first. We must take refuge to heal the past - we must be willing to push through the pain, since pain is where personal growth and healing resides. Without it we continue to conceal the pain by using whatever means to keep us from facing the past. This may mean resorting to stimulants or unconducive behaviour, which act to distract us from the real issue. Once the commitment is made, trust that your healing process had already begun through your willingness to face the past.

Acknowledge the pain: Masking pain may work for the short-term, yet it does not address the underlying issue. It would be akin to applying a band aid to a gushing wound hoping the blood would stop. The deep wound may require stitches and further medical care in order to properly heal. Acknowledging the pain invites you to feel the emotions connected to the pain, rather than stuff them down hoping that it will go away. Remember, *what you resist, persists.* The energy expended towards stuffing down unwanted emotions far exceeds the energy required to heal the emotion. We resist how life should unfold, since we are caught up in a mental and emotional battle to make sense of reality. What if I told you there is another way? What if you did not have to carry the scars of the past with you any longer? Therefore instead of running away from your emotions, lean into them by experiencing them fully. This in itself will transform your fear, anxiety or anger. Let go of what you believe life owes you and step into your challenges. Rise to them armed with courage and a compassionate heart. Maintain confidence that you have been presented with an experience from which to personally evolve.

Acceptance: Everyone encounters pain throughout their life. To sail through life without the contrasting emotional intensities would be to deny your personal growth. Character is formed under difficult circumstances; much like a diamond is formed under heat and pressure. Pain and suffering begins in childhood and continues throughout life. What people do with inner wounds that stem from pain will determine their attitude and actions throughout life. Inner wounds trigger some to persecute themselves. They believe, *"I must deserve this"* or *"I'll never be good enough"* and yet it is this way of thinking that keeps them in a state of unworthiness. We can be hard on ourselves since we fail to respect our past and its accompanying pain need not be viewed as scars any longer. You are not a wounded soul because of your emotional experiences. You become the wounded victim when you repeatedly use those wounds to deflect from attending to the real pain inside. By accepting the past rather than run away from it, you build a bridge, which connects to your future self. The future self delights in bringing you the emotional resources you need to heal this very moment instead of bringing the past and present baggage into the future. Imagine taking a train ride from one side of the country to another and insisting on stopping over in each city to pick up souvenirs. By the end of your journey, not only would you be broke, the amount of energy required to haul your suitcases filled with souvenirs would be physically taxing. So it is with holding on to your pain. Acceptance does not deny you the pain incurred, it merely shines a light on the cracks so as to integrate them back into the wholeness of your being.

Releasing: Notably, Dr John Sarno and Dr Don Colbert have written extensively on how toxic emotions have the capacity to manifest as physical pain. They outline how emotions seek expression through you and if pushed down, will manifest in the body system. Releasing your emotional pain should be met with compassion. You are letting go of the pain and hurt with an open and loving heart in order to cleanse and make peace with the past. The releasing process may be approached in a number of ways. For some, working with a trained mental health professional might be the best decision so as to gently release the pain gradually over time. The skilled professional will deal with each situation individually, as some people may hold deeper emotional wounds than others, especially if there has been physical abuse. Others might turn to a spiritual leader within their community for healing. One's faith in the healing process is paramount and will guide the person to gradually let go and surrender their emotional pain over time. Mixed feelings may surface during the process as well as physical changes in the body, owing to the person purging themselves of the emotional burden carried all these years. Dr Sarno describes healing back pain in hundreds of his patients who conveyed the emotions of anger and anxiety. Similarly Dr Colbert outlined how unforgiveness and betrayal had caused heart disease in a number of his patients who were unwilling to forgive. As you release the emotional wounds of the past, a lightness fills your body and mind – a weight is shifted off your shoulders. This is the weight of carrying the disempowering emotions all this time.

Forgiveness: Whilst we have spoken about the forgiveness process in previous chapters, forgiveness entails forgiving oneself as well as the other person. We are co-creators of our life's experience. Acknowledging this means no longer having to play victim to all that transpires in our life. There is power knowing life need not happen to us, rather that it flows through us. As we create empowering choices that are aligned with our spiritual truth, we trust life functions perfectly within the container of universal wisdom. We have faith that each experience serves a purpose in our personal evolution and once the lesson has been attained, we release and surrender it with openness to what will fill its place. Your belief that you have performed "bad" actions in the past and the ensuing guilt is a flawed assumption, which must be examined. A bad act does not define someone as being bad. Your natural state consists of wholeness and goodness since you were not conceived in the image of evil. It is your thinking that discolours your perception that a bad act in the past must be punished accordingly. Therefore, as you heal the inner conflict contained within the inaccurate belief, you see self-forgiveness is possible and you need not persecute yourself any longer.

Furthermore, if you search deeper within, you will see that your intentions at the time were vested in self-preservation. Our actions arise from the human instinct to take care of oneself at all times, therefore, your actions were imbued with self-love rather than harm to others. Self-forgiveness should be viewed as a process which gradually opens the door to healing and allows us to surrender to life enacting her will through us. We invite the healing energy of love, which resides within us to permeate throughout our being. It is always there, yet we conceal it by perpetuating a false myth of our guilt instead of our innocence.

Letting Go of the Wounded Victim

Letting go of the wounded victim title means to drop the inner dialogue and accompanying behaviour, thus repeating the same victim-like experiences. People who fall into this category of victimhood adopt a passive-aggressive role in their interactions with others. They may pose as victims at times and yet become the aggressor at other times. They are attempting to gain the best of both worlds, since others are more likely to respond to their demands when their behaviour is erratic.

The wounded victim uses blame to deflect feeling bad about oneself. By removing blame for their behaviour, it liberates them from having to identify with the consequences of their actions. They blame others and the world for their current circumstances. They do not assume ownership of their lives since to do so would mean dealing with uncomfortable emotions which threaten their self-esteem. The wounded victim imposes guilt trips on others to lure them into their world so they may feel their pain as well. Much like a spider luring its victim into its web to spin a drama of negativity. Their thought process may correspond to the following inner dialogue, *"If I am to feel miserable, then everyone else must suffer too."* In their best-selling book titled *The Tools*, authors and psychotherapists Phil Stutz and Michels Barry offer the wisdom relating to one's pain story, *"Your experience of pain changes relative to how you react to it. When you move toward it, pain shrinks. When you move away from it, pain grows. If you flee from it, pain pursues you like a monster in a dream."* For the wounded victim, drama is an ever present process playing out their lives, given they are constantly running away from pain since to feel their emotions would be inconceivable.

Playing the victim role elicits sympathy from others towards which they become accustomed to over time. They feed this inner victim every time someone feels pity for them and so the cycle continues. Yet life is not to be lived at this level since this is less than what you are capable of. Unfortunately life's events may lure us into a false security and if we do not attend to our inner life, we find ourselves stuck in this victim role. I know of one such person who has played the victim role for decades. Having known him since early childhood he was dealt a series of unfortunate circumstances, which were not of his choosing. His emotional life was hampered due to parents who were both emotionally distant. Subsequently, he passed through into adulthood and sought to use their external conditions to validate the torment of his inner world. That is, *"I am who I am since my environment has shaped me into this person."* Yet he failed to acknowledge that his thoughts, beliefs and emotions created his external reality which they live today.

To break free from the victimhood role it is crucial to recognise you have been feeding a perpetuating cycle of misery. Take responsibility for your life – owning your problems liberates you from having to blame others for your pain. The problem is never 'out there' and once you appreciate this by connecting with your pain, power is gained knowing you alone create the circumstances of your life. Phil Stutz and Michels Barry remind us once more that, *"Pain is the universe's way of demanding that you continue to learn. The more pain you can tolerate, the more you can learn."*

Own your drama, do not impose it on others in order to appease yourself or to gain something from others. This type of behaviour only perpetuates the victim mentality. Life is replete with wonderful opportunities when we assume ownership of our own circumstances – power and wisdom are summoned when we overcome obstacles rather than cower from them. Change your perception of self so that you cease to identify with the victim. This may be seen as a process rather than an event. It has taken an entire decade of self-development, self-awareness and spiritual guidance to be where I am today and yet my journey of personal growth has only begun. There is no destination to get to in a hurry. Helen Keller reminds us of the virtue of developing character in the following quote, *"Character cannot be developed in ease and quiet. Only through experience of trial and suffering can the soul be strengthened, ambition inspired, and success achieved"*.

Those who play the victim's role must break the cycle of being around people who are also victims. Much like giving up smoking or drinking, disassociate with people who are victims in order to transform the inner self. Many self-help books and courses including A.A. (Alcoholics Anonymous) outline the first steps for healing and transformation begin by distancing oneself from the offending source. It may be hard at first, especially if your source happen to be loved ones or close friends. In time you will come to understand that misery loves company and the more you feed this misery, the more it desires to linger. In chapter three I submitted that you are the sum of the five people whom you regular associate with. If those five people are also victims, your chances of creating an empowering future will be hampered. In a similar vein, take appropriate steps toward becoming the master of your destiny. Undoubtedly you will win some battles in life and lose others. In fact, for a time you may lose more battles than you win, but that is the game of life. It is what you do and whom you become when challenged that determines your character. Everyone can handle winning, there is no lack of feeling good when on top, although not everyone can handle losing and yet it is in losing that our personal character is formed. Seek to develop a deeper understanding of your emotional life, by becoming attuned to your inner dialogue. As you learn to master your emotional life, you will naturally see patterns evolving which give rise to your predominant thoughts. As you tune into these thoughts by observing them, rather than engaging with them, in time they no longer have power over you since you have created a space between them.

Life Doesn't Always Go According to Plan

Letting go of the pain serves to remind us life does not always go according to plan and our best intentions often will not eventuate as we hope. Take a moment to reflect on a situation which failed to turn out as expected – imagine the details as best you can. There may have been an expected outcome you were wishing for. Perhaps you witnessed your well laid-out plans crumble before your very eyes. The premise here is grounded in the knowledge we have the final say in life's unfolding of events. In many ways, suffering is provoked by the assumption we have complete control over our lives. In his book *The Five Things We Cannot Change*, author David Richo suggests we reframe the notion of assuming control by adopting an alternative view, *"we do not let go of control; we let go of the belief we have control."*

The five things we cannot change according to David Richo are depicted in the following conditions:

1. Everything changes and ends.
2. Things do not always go according to plan.
3. Life is not always fair.
4. Pain is a part of life.
5. People are not loving and loyal all the time.

Determinist's and fatalists concede there is a greater force working amid the backdrop of our lives, which is beyond our perspective. We are mere puppets in a well-orchestrated drama of unseen influences acting upon us. Whilst we have free will, ultimately we have very little control once the die is cast. In the book *Way of The Peaceful Warrior*, Dan Millman cleverly highlights the analogy of detachment as a means of surrendering control, *"...once aim is taken and the arrow is loosed from the bow, we can only wait in anticipation to see where it may land."* The notion of control in an ever-changing and expanding universe is irrational in the context of outcomes. Those who seek control realise it is like chasing a stubborn cat. The more you chase the cat, the less likely you will catch it. Through yielding to external forces we allow life to reveal herself through us. We realise that every experience; every thought and emotion is in perfect alignment with the synchronous fulfilment of universal intelligence. The realisation that bad things often happen are beyond the scope of understanding or reason. Yet to hold on to the pain would be to deny the life flowing through us, since resistance is likely to cause more suffering and pain. Therefore, acceptance opens the gateway towards inner peace by allowing pain and suffering to pass through us, rather than remain imbedded in our minds and hearts.

Spiritual masters underscore our unwillingness to conceive life from our hearts. As humanity evolves over the coming millennia, this will become more evident as we awaken our sixth sense – thus attaining spiritual harmony. You need not be spiritually evolved to abide by universal forces. However, aligning with your heart invites you to become acquainted with the silent inner voice within, instead of the egoic mind. Connecting with your heart confers forgiveness is possible despite the belief you have been wronged against and deserving of revenge. Forgiveness is conceivable when we learn to get out of our head and tune into our hearts. It was Blaise Pascal who said, *"The heart has its reasons which reason knows not."* He is reminding us that the heart knows what the conscious mind does not.

In the West, the notion of surrender is met with a sense of hopelessness and vulnerability. It may also be construed for inaction and apathy. It is quite the opposite – letting go of how life should be allows us to consider there is a greater plan unfolding in the backdrop of our lives which we may not fully understand just yet. Surrendering control requires faith and trust. Faith that all your needs will be met once you have resolved to forgive yourself and others and be willing to transform the pain. The power of forgiving and your renewed enthusiasm towards life will reveal itself when the time is right. How can this benevolent universe not honour looking after you? After all, if you are reading this, you have no doubt made it to this point as a result of the choices you made. You have handled every problem, disaster or tragedy and will continue to do so. Faith is comparable to the inner knowing that your heart will pump oxygen-rich blood, with acute precision to your organs every day. You need not be concerned it will not perform its task or that it might oversupply the arteries and organs. It delivers more blood to your working muscles when you exercise and less blood when you are asleep. How does it sense the variation in activity? What is it connected to or receiving instructions in order to manage these resources?

Infinite intelligence has the power and wisdom to function in perfect order and balance once we remove ourselves from constructing drama in our lives.

After all, life is subject to perpetual change based on the law of impermanence. Nothing remains the same, not even the cells in your body, which have a finite lifespan. Knowing this we can take refuge that inner transformation is inexorably linked to the human condition. Rather than oppose it, learn to abide by it. The more you oppose life by holding on to the pain, the less control you have. The essence of this principle is contained in the following passage, *"Life is like sand held in your hands. Held loosely, with an open hand, the sand remains where it is. The minute you close your hand and squeeze tightly to hold on, the sand trickles through your fingers..."* Consequently, rather than clutch tightly, yield to the forces of life - go with the flow. Albeit, this does not imply complete resignation nor indifference. Rather it infers inner detachment. If you feel an inner struggle to let go of your pain for fear of what will fill its place, release your expectation of the outcome by inviting a higher solution to permeate through your life. Rather than surrender to it, yield to life by allowing the situation to lead you where it needs to. Author Susan Gale suggests that when life does not go according to plan, a new and exciting direction may be ahead of us, *"Life doesn't always go according to plan. Sometimes heading in a new direction can be scary until you realize you're headed toward a new and exciting destination."* Sometimes the wrong turn will deliver us to the right place if we are willing to let go of the pain.

CHAPTER 8

What Is Holding You Back?

"Some of us think holding on makes us strong; but sometimes it is letting go."
— *Hermann Hesse*

You cannot put your finger on it, but life has not been the same for as long as you can recall. Mounting pressures may have left you with waned enthusiasm to make things happen. A loss of motivation and an uneasy feeling of being 'stuck' and stagnant fuels your thoughts. Why do we experience episodes of unrest? What could it be calling us to be attentive to? Unrest and inner turmoil is often a calling to attend to an aspect of our inner self that we have disassociated with. The more we stray from our authentic self, the greater the emotional demands become apparent as we attempt to reconcile with our deepest nature.

Your problems are an invitation to deal with the disowned aspects of you. Therefore, problems become opportunities if we recognise them as such by being attentive to lessons contained within the painful experiences.

Assuming control of your life should not be defined by an external change in circumstances, rather it requires a resetting of your internal compass. The decision to create a new blueprint for your life must come from a deep desire to change for the better. The Freudian psychological principle, known as the "Pain-Pleasure" principle states that humans have an inner drive toward seeking pleasure, or conversely running away from pain. You either attract opportunities that serve your highest potential or get stuck in a painful cycle of undesired outcomes. The downfall of the pain cycle is that you learn to model the behaviour of lab mice given electric shock treatment. It has been reported that over time, mice become addicted to pain as a result of the electric shock and thus a vicious circle ensues. In order to take control of your life, take ownership of your thoughts, choices and actions. We are solely responsible for steering the course of our destiny. As to which channel your ship ventures depends on the forces of life. Your task is to orientate yourself in the right direction while continuing to advance forward, despite the consequences of life.

I invite you to examine the following points relating to areas of your life that may demand your attention. How do you know? If you identify with any of these points, there is a good chance that attribute is at play in your life. As you read through these points be truthfully honest with yourself and do not shy away and identify with the trait. In order to heal and transform our pain, we must be willing to face our fear and obstacles with an open mind and a compassionate heart. Be aware of any critical inner dialogue which may surface as you read through the points. Do not label or judge yourself – like a detective you are merely identifying areas of your life that warrant your attention. This will become crucial in part two of the book as we undertake to create an empowering life path for your future.

Fear of the unknown: Familiarity can be comforting. We may become accustomed to a particular way of life, therefore initiating a much needed change - difficult at the best of times. Life can be bumpy, so why rock the boat and risk the consequences that accompany change? It is for this reason relationship experts suggest men and women prefer to stay in toxic relationships rather than risk being alone. Do you cower from opportunities which compromise your comfort level?

Fear of pain: Fear of pain stops us dead in our tracks – after all who wants to constantly butt heads against painful events. What areas of your emotional life do you fear coming to terms with?

Impaired self-belief: Have you adopted other people's beliefs, especially family. While they may be well-intended, if they do not serve your growth, they could be holding you back. During our formative years, embracing our parents' beliefs are unavoidable. As we mature into adults we have the capacity to examine those beliefs to determine whether they are self-serving.

Disempowering thoughts: The same habitual thoughts day in and day out create a reality based on the sum of those thoughts. Being mindful and attentive to your thoughts consistently weeds out any negative thinking bias. Are you aware of your habitual negative thought patterns, if any?

Restrictive habits: Destructive habits may become embedded into the subconscious mind and have the potential to wreak havoc in your life if unexamined. If you are unconscious of your habits, you are running on autopilot, drawing the same undesired circumstances in to your life. Spiritual leaders call it being 'asleep.' Owing to mindful awareness, it is possible to create a fresh outlook as you become aware of your limitations. What restrictive habits would you like to overcome? Overeating, gossiping, negative thinking, etc.

Blame: Blaming others and the conditions of your life reaffirms a victim temperament. The problem is always 'out there', and not within your power to make the necessary changes. Whilst you have little control how life's events transpire, you have the wherewithal to respond to those events and circumstances with integrity. Power is attained amid awareness and right action. Are you constantly blaming others and the world for your current state of affairs?

Lack of resources and knowledge: Lack of resources and information may hold people back, particularly with respect to one's career choices. It is estimated in these rapidly advancing times, what was relevant fourteen months ago is no longer appropriate today. Therefore, remaining abreast of current trends is a vital requirement in your professional affairs. Continued learning through regular reading or attending courses allows you to stay ahead. Are there areas of your professional life that need attention? What steps can you take immediately?

Elevated expectations: You may carry expectations of yourself, others and even life. When your expectations do not externalise as expected, you feel victimised. Let go of the HOW's and WHAT's of your expectations, while considering that everything you need reaches you at the right time, as you align with your deepest desires. Do you have unrealistic expectations of people or circumstances unfolding in your life?

How Beliefs Create Your Reality

As you explore aspects of your life that may be holding you back, the power of your beliefs is an integral component which holds the key to your potential. Beliefs form the foundation to a wish, a prayer or an intention and may be clothed with a powerful will and desire. The Free Online Dictionary defines beliefs as the *mental acceptance of and conviction in the truth, actuality, or validity of something.* My own definition embraces the principle of truth despite evidence proving otherwise. I would like to outline the case of how beliefs have the power to create your reality in the following section. Why have I chosen to focus on beliefs to highlight those aspects which may be holding you back?

Consider the last time you applied for job or were planning on purchasing a car, home or anything of considerable value. Your belief in the occurrence unfolding in a well-orchestrated manner is a powerful tool which shapes your coming reality. Often, we have no idea how we know what we know, yet it is more than that – it is an inner knowing met with a strong conviction that events will come to pass in a positive way. We do not need to know the precise details how events will unfold, yet our inner guidance affirms the belief that all will be well if we proceed with an open mind and a welcoming heart. Call it gut instinct, sixth sense or an inner knowing, beliefs serve to reaffirm your connection to a greater intelligence. You co-create life when you follow and act on your beliefs. Your beliefs have power through the thoughts and emotions you entrust them with. Recall a time when you really believed in a cause with all your heart and soul. How did your body feel? You may have experienced an inner peace and tranquillity wash over you, despite an outward appearance or lack of physical evidence. This is the power of belief working through you.

Personally, I hold the empowering belief which affirms, *every event has the potential to shape my life when I choose to be receptive to the lessons which unfolds*. With this in mind, I suspend my judgement about what life should look like, by becoming aware and receptive to the infinite intelligence and wisdom which resides within me. I turn down the volume on my ego, which seeks to reaffirm its own plan and choose to allow spirit to co-create my destiny. I discover opportunities that become readily available when I adopt this way of thinking, rather become embroiled in negative thoughts. I create and shape my reality based on infinite love, not fear. I believe in an intelligent and supreme force, one that guides my steps. I reason this force was responsible for creating a benevolent universe which continues to support me. Your soul knows what is right for you – it has no agenda other than your personal evolution and happiness though the fulfilment of your deepest desires.

Your beliefs are powerful and colour every experience by intensifying your perception of reality. You are the creator of your life. You are the story teller, the director and producer of your destiny. You do not have to know the infinite details of how life will unfold. You simply **believe** life is serving you and will continue to do so as long as you allow life to flow through you. How can it not? Remember, I posed the question a few pages back; how can the same force that gave you life not support your growth, happiness and wellbeing? Your choices are influenced by your beliefs, be it right or wrong. It is for this reason you become empowered though personal growth to take ownership by making conscious choices. You are invited to become *aware* and *awake*. This does not mean sailing through life impervious to your choices and actions. Many people blindly act out their subconscious beliefs and wonder why their life is not what they imagined it to be.

Take a moment to examine the following questions by journaling your answers on paper. Go with the first insights that come to mind. Do not dwell too much on looking for the right answers, since you will become caught in a flurry of thoughts. Connect to your thoughts through feeling your way through the process. Awareness is the first step toward change.

Have you formed beliefs through the influence of others?
If so, whom? Family, friends, work colleagues, teachers, sports coaches, ministers or that of your collective society?
How are they serving you right now?
If they are not serving you, which beliefs do you need to re-examine and change to support your future?

Examine aspects of your life which you may have formed inaccurate representations. Consider the *quality* of your life. Not quantity, which is measured by material possessions. Look at the value of the beliefs you create.

When did you form those beliefs?
What was occurring in your life around the time these beliefs were formed?

In his book *The Power of Belief*, author Ray Dodd provides us with four steps to follow in order to change a belief. These are:

Practise awareness: Remove yourself from what is familiar or 'known.' These are beliefs formed long ago which may no longer serve you now. Challenge the inner voice that demands that it has to be this way. This inner critic may arise when you challenge an existing belief. Silence the monkey mind; the endless chatter which seeks to interpret every action, thought and event.

Give up the need to be right: Relinquish beliefs which no longer serve you. In surrendering those beliefs, you suspend the need to gather evidence though justification to prove you are right. As you become aware, notice how needing to be right feels. Is it empty inside, as though an inner voice is asking you to let it go? By resisting gathering evidence, you let go of your attachment to your 'old story.'

Create a new dream: Design a new agreement which re-works the old belief. After you have challenged the old belief, formulate a new and empowering belief which resonates with you. Following on from my earlier example my new belief became, *I stand in my own power and I know my true worth*. It encompassed the qualities I felt were essential for living in alignment with my higher self. Gather evidence to support your new belief. Begin living it, breathing it and being it.

Examine your beliefs by becoming aware of if they are serving you right now. You need not adopt other people's ideas or beliefs, believing that since they work for them, they will serve you too. Allow your true self to unfold; since the life of your dreams awaits you on the other side. It already exists *out there...*just tune into it!

Overcoming Obstacles

In keeping with the notion of exploring aspects of your life that holds you back, here is a short story that illustrates how our desire to overcome obstacles may be the single biggest hurdle we can overcome to create a compelling future.

"In ancient times, a King had a boulder placed on a roadway. Then hiding, he watched to see if anyone would remove the huge rock. Some of the King's wealthiest merchants and courtiers came by and simply walked around it. Many loudly blamed the King for not keeping the roads clear, but none did anything about getting the stone out of the way.

But then a peasant came along, carrying a load of vegetables. Upon approaching the boulder, the peasant laid down his burden and tried to move the stone to the side of the road. After much pushing and straining, he finally succeeded.

After the peasant picked up his load of vegetables, he noticed a purse lying in the road where the boulder had been. The purse contained many gold coins and a note from the King indicating that the gold was for the person who removed the boulder from the roadway.

The peasant learned what many of us will never understand: Every obstacle presents an opportunity to improve our condition.

What may often appear as an obstacle holding us back, can in fact become an opportunity for our greatest triumph. You see, it is in the way we approach our obstacles and frame the situation which determines our progress. If you believe an obstacle is a dead-end, you find every reason to substantiate this by falling victim to the forces acting upon you. On the other hand, if you acknowledge the obstacle by coming to terms with the likelihood that it is presenting you with a valuable opportunity to grow and expand, you will naturally call upon your inner resources to navigate your way through.

It was Albert Einstein who said, *"The world we have made, as a result of the level of thinking we have done thus far, creates problems we cannot solve at the same level of thinking at which we created them."* He was reinforcing the idea that you do not overcome obstacles with a fixed or limited mindset, since this is the same mind which created the problem in the first instance. We must transcend our problems by looking at them with a new mind, a fresh and open approach. I am reminded of the Thomas Dewar quote echoed in the sentiment to keep our minds open and receptive to new ideas and information, *"Minds are like parachutes; they work best when open."* Overcoming obstacles offers us the freedom to live our highest potential by breaking new ground and extending our inner resolve. We grow more when more is asked of us – it is in reaching where human growth resides, for our setback have been put before us not to dishearten us, rather to thrive and reach beyond our capabilities.

The following principles serve as a guide in areas of your life which may be holding you back. Obstacles can thwart our success or elevate us to new heights. Examine them by reflecting on their symbolic meaning to your life. Be willing to abandon endeavours that do not deliver results. Far too many people discount the value of redirecting their attention elsewhere when all attempts have been exhausted. Pride, self-worth and time invested are the main reasons cited for flogging a dead horse.

Distance yourself emotionally: When faced with an obstacle, emotions run high as you typically react to the ensuing drama. Step back mentally and emotionally by viewing the obstacle from a greater perspective. An accomplished Australian artist, noted for her oil painting, prefers to take regular breaks throughout the painting process. This allows her to return to her work with a fresh set of eyes and approach painting from a completely different vantage point. You might adopt the same approach with your obstacle – take a break from it for a while, returning with renewed enthusiasm when the time is right.

Seek out necessary resources: Often, you may be lacking certain provisions, finances, strategies or a key piece of knowledge to conquer your obstacle. The key is to acknowledge your obstacle as you may be *resource dependant*. For example, you may require a key software program to automate a process, freeing you to direct your attention to more important work. Consult with those who can help you move through the hurdle. As they say, enlist a fresh pair of eyes to see what you may be lacking.

Gain perspective: It can be overwhelming when an unforeseen obstacle emerges. Getting caught up in the ensuing crisis redirects vital resources required to make critical decisions. Gaining perspective allows you to step away from the 'noise'. You might seek help from others, talk to friends or loved ones who may offer a different assessment of your challenge. Perspective does not imply distancing yourself in apathy. It simply means viewing the obstacle from numerous vantage points while considering other options.

Evaluate the obstacle: Can something be done now to overcome the obstacle or does it require specialised assistance? Consider the obstacle objectively as though you were seeing it for the first time. Engage your logical mind by applying sound judgement to the task ahead. Avoid becoming emotionally invested while enslaved to the task.

Remain focussed and committed: Sometimes an obstacle is not intended to weaken your endeavours. Perhaps, it is an invitation to get clear on the process in order to progress to the next stage. It is advising you to attend to a particular aspect now, rather than in the future when you have invested valuable time and energy.

Be unrelenting in your commitment: Do not give up. Do not allow setbacks to get you down. You are bound to fall upon many setbacks in life. Obstacles help enrich your mental experience in so far as building resilience, fortitude and strength. Every time you tackle a problem, you overcome a mental hurdle.

Develop a growth mindset: In her book *Mindset: The New Psychology of Success*, author Carol Dweck delves deep into the two different mindsets required for success: fixed or growth focussed mindsets. She provides the reader with a comprehensive foundation for developing a growth mindset, which is aspiring toward continuous improvement and building on your successes. She reminds us, *"The passion for stretching yourself and sticking to it, even (or especially) when it's not going well, is the hallmark of the growth mindset. This is the mindset that allows people to thrive during some of the most challenging times in their lives."*

Failure Is Not an Option, It's a Prerequisite

Having examined a plan for overcoming obstacles and the number of ways to reframe our obstacles, let us look at how the fear of failure can hold us back. Why are people so scared of failure? Where in our personal history did we first subscribe to the notion that failing is bad? You might be inclined to cite the obvious answer - *it prevents me from getting what I want. It makes me feel unworthy or hopeless. It moves me further away from what I really want.* The underlying aspect behind failure is the meaning you assign to what failure represents. Yet that's what it took to invent the electric light bulb. Edison's quote, which has become testament for the power of persistence signifies the truth of his reality, *"I have not failed. I've just found 10,000 ways that won't work."* Thomas Edison reframed failure to mean something greater. His declaration that it took 10,000 attempts to create something which previously did not exist highlights the growing need to develop persistence, rather than concede to failure.

What if to create a vision of something greater required continual failure to get it right? Would you still proceed despite this? Tony Robbins suggests failure is *an undesired outcome*. I find this an ingenious approach, since at times we want to control things that are beyond the scope of our control. He furthermore reminds us that failure is a teaching tool and may often delay your progress leading to something greater, *"I've come to believe that all my past failure and frustration were actually laying the foundation for the understandings that have created the new level of living I now enjoy."* If you hold a big dream or ambition for your future, failure is inevitable. I am yet to stumble across historical literature connecting those who succeeded with an invention, goal or dream in their first attempt. Leonardo da Vinci was one such exemption since he created many inventions in his mind. He used the power of imagination and creativity to bring to life numerous inventions in what he called thought experiments. *He* reasoned that once it is created at the level of the mind, bringing it to life becomes second nature. Whilst there have been few geniuses to rival Leonardo da Vinci , his biographer noted the countless hours he spent tirelessly fine tuning his inventions to bring them to life.

Our human nature lends itself to failure. There are numerous unknown variables beyond our control which hinder progress. Although the greatest men in history have been able to master their thoughts, few of us have the ability to harness the power of our mind like a laser beam. Our thoughts ultimately influence our success in life. When we co-create with universal forces, it takes the burden off needing to be exact, perfect and hard on ourselves. The concept of failure is diminished since there is no timing or deadline to *get it right* the first time. I would like you to consider reframing the notion of failure by not connecting it to lack of self-worth. Whatever endeavour you face, view it from a higher perspective. By that I mean; if you were the universe looking down on yourself, what advice or counsel would you give? Personally, when I adopt this way of thinking, I reassure myself with the silent mantra – *You're right on track, go easy on yourself.* When we remove guilt or pressure from ourselves, we give permission for our unique talents, skills and geniuses to be revealed. This energy is a consciousness which knows all. Align yourself with this energy using your unconscious mind to help you steer a path toward the answer.

How can you achieve this state of expansive awareness in the context of overcoming what is holding you back? I suggest relating it to the areas of your life that matters most by refining any aspect which does not serve you. Some years ago I scaled back on working with individual clients to focus more on speaking, writing and coaching. At first I was a little anxious I had made the wrong decision, since I took a pay cut to pursue my passion. Similarly there were no guarantees it was going to pay off and I was in no position to supplement the lost income, at least until the new business venture turned profitable. Upon first impressions, I become aware of the spare time that was now available to me in the afternoon. Fatigue set in during the afternoon owing to a change in routine from standing to sitting, which I was not accustomed to. I used this down time as it were, to take advantage of a twenty minute nap due to weariness. This change in routine initially took me by surprise since I thought I was dropping off my work commitments, yet I was genuinely tired from sitting at a computer all day instead of actively working out with clients occasionally, which is what I was accustomed to.

Over time I noted that during these twenty minute *intervals*, some of my greatest ideas for articles, projects and business ideas emerged. I went so far as to leave a notepad beside my bed in order to jot down thoughts and ideas which emerged during that brief interlude. Upon further research, the brief naps offered me an opportunity to harness deep subconscious realisations that were not apparent when I was awake. Have you noticed that when you are in a stressed state, being creative is impossible? This is due to the shutting down of the left brain, which is the seat of logic. The right brain is intuitive, holistic and creative. Using this practice allowed me to push through failure by viewing it from a different perspective. Invariably, in time gone by I would have ruminated at my desk seeking answers with little success. By transitioning into a conducive, subconscious state my mind found the best way to harness its creative ability.

Consider the following points as a means to overcome failure.

- Find a unique way to harness your potential that contradicts what society imposes upon us. It might involve taking a nap at the middle point of the way, a walk, down time while relaxing in nature, meditation or time alone in deep contemplation. Experiment with the process until you establish a routine which serves you well. A word of advice – being in a relaxed state harnesses the power of your parasympathetic system, otherwise known as the rest or digest branch of the ANS (Autonomic Nervous System). Going into deeper relaxed states not only is conducive to fostering Alpha brain wave states, but it has also been shown to reduce the stress hormone cortisol over time.

- Reframe the concept of failure to a more empowering state, rather than the loss of something. When we view failure as a process which brings us closer to our intended outcomes, it releases the pressure from having to get things right or the need for perfection. Oftentimes, the end result may hinge on a number of repeated failures, which draw you closer to you desired outcome. Therefore, do not have a fixed mindset toward how life should unfold or what constitutes success. Hold off defining outcomes arising to your current circumstances. Life's events have an uncanny way of taking shape when you least expect it.

- Remove the pressure from holding a fixed outcome. An outcome already exists out there within the realm of universal intelligence. The universe holds multiple ways of achieving an outcome if your intentions and convictions are firm. Release your expectations of life events to unfold naturally. Expectations limit the flow of the experience. We add layers to our experience of life to rationalise the world, albeit at a cost by limiting our perspective. In his interview with Oprah Winfrey, Brazilian author Paulo Coelho who wrote *The Alchemist*, attributes his success to being open and receptive to uncertainty. He reminds us to flow through life – allowing it to carry you where it needs to be devoid of expectations, anxiety or frustration. As we gain trust in the rhythm of life, we acquire confidence through our attentiveness to the signs life bestows us. So how can we liberate ourselves from expectations while fulfilling our human needs? Firstly, experience the world through the eyes of a child. Surrender all expectations as you remain fascinated by uncertainty and ambiguity, which are the birthplace of creation. Secondly, stay grounded and present – this allows you to let go of future expectations and the need to recycle the past in to the present moment. Remaining present invites you to embody life's experiences with fullness.

You draw closer to your desired outcome every time you fail. Learn to embrace failure as a necessary step forward, not a stop sign. Trust that every time you fail, the process reveals itself a little more. Your greatest victory will come when you cooperate with the power of your mind, for your greatest ally has a supreme intelligence capable of the right answers. When you accept there are no such thing as failure, progress and success will be ready to greet you. Knowing this, failure is not an option – it's a prerequisite.

Giving Up Is Not an Option

Until now we have examined a number of ideas relating to areas of your life that may be limiting your progress in some way. We considered a number of possibilities at the beginning of this chapter that might be imposing upon your success. We then ventured into the power of beliefs by examining the ways beliefs can also hold you back and hamper your progress. I questioned you to reflect in order to gain a clear-cut understanding of the areas of life that needed your attention. Similarly, I outlined the case for how beliefs shape and create your reality. Consequently, it stands to reason that if we possess inaccurate beliefs about reality, it is likely we will draw those experiences into our life – *as within, so without* goes the axiom. We also observed the essential aspects for helping you overcome limiting beliefs as outlined by author Ray Dodd in his book *The Power of Belief.* Finally, we studied a number of approaches to overcome obstacles which may be holding you back. These points are crucial for helping you come to terms with the answers to the questions I posed in that section pertaining to the nature of your beliefs.

In this final chapter of Part 1, I wish to make the case for why giving up should never be entertained as long as you hold a clear vision of your dreams. I should preface this section by declaring my fascination with billionaires, which has been apparent for some time. Allow me to explain in more detail how my fascination extends to more than the mere accumulation of wealth; for that is just the tip of the iceberg. I must assert the obvious that my curiosity extends towards the **mindset** of self-made billionaires as opposed to their net worth or material wealth. Consider the conviction a self-made billionaire has in order to reach their level of success, notwithstanding the insurmountable hurdles along the way. Whilst researching this topic in 2011, there were 946 billionaires in the world. At the time of writing this, that number had swelled to 1,645 with an aggregate wealth of $6.4 trillion. That is a staggering number. Despite people's beliefs about the rich, the wealthy are not deceitful in their pursuit of wealth – rather they are astute and industrious. To become a billionaire requires overcoming numerous mental and emotional hurdles. It requires a **profound confidence** to never give up, given that the economic forces of life are continually against those reaching for success.

In order to attain an astounding level of wealth, one must **think and act differently**. There must be an inherent **self-belief**, an unyielding motivation and a desire to prevail. Represented in the quote, *"The more you help people get what they want, the more you get what you want,"* is the basis to a wealthy person's philosophy. Self-made billionaires maintain an unwavering level of mental toughness and resiliency. According to leading authors who have written about talent and success, including: Malcom Gladwell, Cal Newport and Robert Greene; talent is not bestowed upon us at the time of our birth. Rather, success is acquired over time, arising from firm persistence and dedication. Whilst the nature vs nurture discussion has eluded scientists and behavioural economists for years, many have struggled to draw a consensus on what it takes to be talented. In recent times, evolutionary psychologists now infer that nurture nature is a more appropriate term, which suggests that environment accounts for a large portion of a person's success, whilst acknowledging DNA to be equally important.

In keeping with success as a motivating factor, the following points are valuable models for building a resiliency mindset and thus eliminating the need to *give up*:

- A relentless desire to succeed.
- Extending yourself each time.
- Enjoying the journey.

Let us examine each point in greater detail:

A relentless desire to succeed: Recall the last time you learned something new. You might have reached a point and proclaimed, *"To hell with this, I give up"*. I know I have. I would like to reframe the concept of winning to include, **NOT giving up** despite outward appearances. Leadership expert and author Robin Sharma offers the following sage advice, *"If people aren't laughing at you at least once a week, your dreams are too small."* That is, you are not reaching beyond your capabilities. Often, you may expect to reap the rewards for the hard work you earned. There may be little indication of progress for weeks, months or years. You may even become disheartened at this stage and give up; right when a breakthrough is imminent. This is an all too common scenario for most people. We strive for external confirmation, believing the fruits of our labour will ultimately yield a positive sign. At this crucial point, we need to trust that events are unfolding in our favour behind the scenes and beyond our limited senses. The aphorism which invites you to *believe it before you see it* underscores the message of deep optimism.

Extending yourself each time: A number of people succumb to the impression they must put everything on the line in order to thrive and prosper; that they must sacrifice everything in the pursuit of their dreams. This is a misleading assumption based on a number of reasons. Steady improvements over time often yield greater returns. Whilst I am not advocating a new idea, it was author Darren Hardy who skilfully outlines this point in his prize winning book, *Compound Effect*. Using the elastic band as a metaphor; your aim should be to extend yourself a little further each time, beyond your comfort zone. In doing so you discover more about yourself while taking calculated risks, since you are able to identify mistakes with an enriched mind.

Enjoying the journey: In refusing to give up, you reconnect with your underlying motivation for pursuing your dream in the first place. Having become clear on your purpose, savouring the journey becomes the ultimate aphrodisiac. I frequently work twelve hour days including weekends with adequate rest and exercise in-between. As Sunday arrives, I often reflect on what I have achieved during the week and how I can build on my success in the following week. It is reassuring to note that I have not really worked at all – I have simply been absorbed in a flow experience called work, which I remain deeply passionate about. Similarly, I invite you to find your passion and pursue it with gusto – let the spirit of your quest come alive through you.

I trust these points have served to reignite your desire to move forward with enthusiasm by compelling you not to give up. Failure is one thing and as outlined in previous chapters, it is merely the opportunity to get it right on your next attempt. However, giving up should be your last and final resort once you have exhausted all avenues. Giving up routes a message to the brain whilst impressing upon it the notion of futility and hopelessness. Your mind becomes astute at learning this model of behaviour and uses it against you on your next pursuit. What causes some people to pursue their dreams with vehement desire while others give up when the going gets tough? Having studied a number of successful people over the years, an **insatiable hunger to succeed** is a common thread leading toward success. Successful people are unrelenting toward the pursuit of their dreams. Certainly they experience setbacks and failures like everyone else. What sets them apart though is the ability to bounce back and learn from their mistakes. It is the ability to do this time and time again until they succeed, which sets them apart from others who fail.

Successful people believe in themselves. They have developed an inner resolve – an inner dialogue that feeds them with successful images, thoughts and beliefs. This inner dialogue has the power to cancel out any external reservations that arise in the pursuit of their dreams. Equally I suggest you find your inner conviction and unearth your underlying reason for pursuing your dreams. Why do you want it so bad? Who will you become once you have attained this way of life? What will life look like when you have attained your dreams? Model the people who have accomplished a similar dream and pursue it with passion. Successful people are adaptable. They know what they want. They are open and receptive to allowing life to show them the how-to. When you develop an undying commitment toward a dream, roadblocks and failures become speed humps instead of stop signs. Your dream should be so great that it feeds and ignites your soul with purpose and meaning. You embody the dream in every cell of your being so that you become **inspired** to attain it, rather than motivated, since motivation tends to wane as we encounter obstacles and challenges. Inspiration sets a dream on fire and maintains it over time.

As a final thought, an unrelenting persistence and dedication were also hailed as defining attributes of successful people. With that in mind, create a vision of your ideal future. Fill it with optimism and empowering beliefs owing to your overall success – never give up, since you never know when the tides of fortune will come your way.

Life can serve you in a number of ways if you remain receptive to the forces acting upon you. What may often appear as your worst nightmare, often transforms into your greatest lesson. My personal life is testament to this. As I outlined in my previous book *The Power to Navigate Life: Your Journey to Freedom*, my own health crisis and the death of my father led me to seek answers to my questions as to why people get sick. I continued searching for answers for a number of years to solve my own health concerns before realising I was living the answers. Life had shown me the path to solve my questions through the power of seeking a higher solution. You do not have to remain a prisoner to the past any longer. If you seek to live your life imbued with meaning and purpose, it is vital that you make peace with the past. The previous chapters outlined essential elements for navigating your way towards freedom.

I will draw this section to a close by recapping some of the main points for you to reflect on.

Accept Yourself As You Are

Instead of viewing yourself as damaged goods, strive to accept yourself exactly as you are. This does not underscore the need for continual self-improvement, yet it flies in the face of disowning aspects of yourself that you dislike. Accepting yourself as you are means embracing the darkness and the light – the Shadow Self. To focus only on your imperfections underscores the uniqueness of your other qualities. By focussing on your weaknesses, you give them energy and power over you. You identify with your shortcomings, rather than see them as one aspect of your being. As you embrace them they meld into the light of your being.

You Are Exactly Where You Are Meant To Be

Your life need not be a struggle. Your problems are opportunities if you allow them to be. Stop your destructive and distorted thinking which tells you the world should be a certain way; that life owes you something or people must fulfil your standards. Accept 'things' just the way they are; since that is **exactly** how they are. Your need to make things fit your mould is the cause of your suffering. I am not suggesting you accept less than you deserve. I suggested you become awake and aware in order that you become the **navigator** of your own life; willing to sail into any type of condition. Too often, people view life's ordeals as unwelcomed. To the enlightened, it is viewed as a gift; a valuable lesson. The lexicon *How may I use this lesson to my advantage?* becomes an empowering reflection to view your role as co-creator of your life.

Your Past Does Not Define You, It Shapes You

Accepting that life can be challenging at times, allows us to surrender with an affirmation of complete acceptance, rather than suffer. Saying yes to the circumstances that transpire in no way underscores their impact on your life. It is merely an inner declaration that everything will turn out alright in the end. It is in no way conceding in apathy as you might believe. Challenges are an invitation to accept change in your life. If there is resistance to the change, suffering is brought on from your unwillingness to embrace what unfolds. You would agree that life is subject to constant change. What unfolds during the initial stages of a significant life change may not be in agreement with what you had anticipated. Hence, it is the uncertainty of the change which leaves you gasping for breath, rather than the change itself. Your response to embracing life's challenges is to lean into them with compassion and an open heart. Remember, your resistance creates more resistance, thus leading to more suffering. Leaning in to your challenges is a mental and emotional confirmation to yield to the resistance by embracing what develops.

There Are No Mistakes

As we learn to embrace what is, we surrender the need to create our own story and drama, which we believe is better than what is unfolding in our external reality. Accepting the perfection of this present moment allows you to let go of needing to change anything out there. However, this does not mean that you surrender in apathy, it means that you offer less resistance to the forces of life, knowing that everything taking place in your life is part of your personal evolution. Embrace life by perceiving it as a practice, much like sitting meditation or exercise. The more you practice the better you become. Your mental and emotional states become attuned to offering less resistance through an awareness to the present moment. The practice of embracing life means that at times you will naturally slip up. This should be an opportunity to practice self-directed compassion and instead be less critical of yourself, since you are learning a new language.

Make Peace with the Past

Everyone has a past and in that past are most likely painful memories, disappointments and frustrations. Many people cope with the negative emotions which accompany the painful experiences, but there are many that do not cope in a positive way. There is a tendency to stow the pain where it gets locked in the subconscious mind. This negative energy buried deep down may stay there for a while, but eventually it tries to surface so that it can be dealt with. It is there lying beneath the surface since emotions are simply energy in motion which need to be expressed. The repressed emotion will manifest in certain ways and at certain times until it is dealt with. Healing the past and the pain associated with it is vital to overcoming the pain by recognising you have stored your pain down deep throughout the years. The mind is astute at protecting you and unwittingly you may bury the pain in an attempt to dispose of the feelings and emotions associated with the experience.

Lessons on Forgiveness

The key to working through self-punishment is to recognise that our thoughts are deeply ingrained, having been reinforced over many years. It will require concentrated effort and patience to move through this phase of reconciliation. Changing your inner dialogue to being pleasant overnight may be seen as a threat to the ego, since you have become accustomed to the voice of the inner critic. Positive self-talk in this instance may be akin to speaking in another tongue. Whilst the nature of the self-directed inner talk may be familiar, it does not feel true since you have grown accustomed to the self-punishing talk over time. In a previous chapter I outlined how guilt imposes itself in such a way to appease ourselves for wrongful actions. We unconsciously punish ourselves since this is viewed as self-retribution for untoward action in the past. People at this level who typically feel bad about themselves will develop a harsh inner critic who feels compelled to punish oneself for wrongful acts.

Letting Go Of the Pain

It takes a great deal of energy to keep the past alive. The mental and emotional resources required could be better spent on other rewarding life experiences. Over time, if left untreated, painful memories have the capacity to transform into psychosomatic illnesses. Mental health professionals believe it takes approximately one and a half minutes for the body to process an emotion. Knowing this, we need not hold onto mental and emotional pain from the past, nor do we need to carry it with us for years. Simply dealing with the emotion as it arises allows it to move through the body in a shorter amount of time and without the long term physiological effects. Often, people hold on to their pain for so long that it forms a safety blanket. They would feel lost without the pain and suffering. After all, they would have no story to tell. Perhaps others might find them uninteresting. Who would they be without their story?

What Is Holding You Back?

Your problems are an invitation to deal with the disowned aspects of you. Therefore, problems become opportunities if we recognise them as such by being attentive to lessons contained within the painful experiences. Assuming control of your life should not be defined by an external change in circumstances, rather it requires a resetting of your internal compass. The decision to create a new blueprint for your life must come from a deep desire to change for the better. The Freudian psychological principle known as the Pain-Pleasure principle states that humans have an inner drive toward seeking pleasure or conversely running away from pain. You either attract opportunities that serve your highest potential or get stuck in a painful cycle of undesired outcomes. In order to take control of your life, take ownership of your thoughts, choices and actions. We are solely responsible for steering the course of our destiny. As to which channel your ship ventures on depends on the forces of life. Your task is to orientate yourself in the right direction while continuing to advance forward, despite the consequences of life.

The key lessons contained within Part I is that of inviting peace to a troubled past by being attentive to your emotional life. Problems do not arise **out there** in your external reality. Problems start within and subsequently manifest into something greater in your reality, since you have lost touch with your inner sense of peace. It is worth mentioning again, "*As within, so without.*" This simple axiom underscores the need to strike at the root of the problem by healing our inner life. As we make peace within, our external reality coincides to reflect the changes. Have you noticed how monks, yogis and spiritual gurus seem to be in a constant state of peace and calm? Coincidentally, their external reality also reflects this inner peace and rarely is there an event or situation which disrupts their inner peace. The Navy Seals have a saying, *calm is contagious.* As you work toward gaining inner peace, your so-called problems no longer dominate your thoughts. Rather, you create a peaceful inner haven in which to connect with life.

In Part II of the book, we will be taking a journey towards creating a new and remarkable future by using the principles and lessons attained in Part I. You cannot live a compelling future if you drag the past with you. It is vital that you attend to the past in order to make peace with it and leave it where it belongs – behind you. You may have heard the aphorism which states, *though your body is here, your mind is somewhere else.* To create a remarkable future worth looking forward to, reconnect with the present moment where your body resides and create the future with a sincere and honest presence to be here and now where life serves you in all her glory.

PART 2
CREATE A REMARKABLE FUTURE

CHAPTER 9

Rewrite a New Life Script

Finding Your Life's Purpose

"When you see what you're here for, the world begins to mirror your purpose in a magical way. It's almost as if you suddenly find yourself on a stage in a play that was written expressly for you." — Betty Sue Flowers

In his book, *The Power of Purpose*, author Richard J. Leider offers readers an insightful story for finding one's purpose through action: "A young man who was searching for his life's purpose wrote to Rabbi Menachem Mendel Schneerson. He said he had discussed the purpose question with every wise person he had come across, had read every book on purpose he could find and had travelled to faraway places to seek the guidance of some of the greatest spiritual teachers. However, no one had ever been able to tell him what his purpose was.

So he asked the rabbi, "Can you tell me what my purpose in life is?"

Rabbi Schneerson responded, "By the time you figure out what your mission is, you will have no time to fulfil it."

This simple story demonstrates the growing plight of many to search for their purpose outside of themselves, while it remains within all along. It was Gandhi who reminded us that your purpose is defined by enhancing the lives of others, *"The best way to find yourself is to lose yourself in the service of others."* In a slightly different vein, author Steven Pressfield in his acclaimed book, *The War of Art*, offers us an alternative perspective on seeking purpose. He cleverly highlights the inherent struggle to break down the barriers of resistance, which is a common experience that accompanies the creative process, *"Because when we sit down day after day and keep grinding, something mysterious starts happening. A process is set into motion by which, inevitably and infallibly, heaven comes to our aid. Unseen forces enlist in our cause; serendipity reinforces our purpose."*

Your life's purpose is found through trial and effort. Purpose is found in action, not inaction. I intentionally titled this section 'finding' your life purpose, since I believe it to be an ongoing process throughout one's life. Your purpose may vary and serve others in numerous ways as you evolve. Be mindful of solely attaching your purpose to your career however, evident when one is made redundant or their company downsizes. Many people describe feelings of emptiness following an unexpected change in their profession, since they have unwittingly connected their purpose to their career. Moreover, the notion you have ONE purpose in life remains a misconception undeserving of your attention. There are numerous stories of successful people who have found innumerable callings throughout their life.

In his book, *The Undefeated Mind*, Dr Alex Lickerman recounts the story of a woman, who after nursing her sick husband, succeeds in finding meaning and purpose by dedicating herself to the terminally ill, following his death. While suffering bouts of depression and guilt in the wake of his loss, the strain imposed upon her caring for him in the final moments of his life were too much to bear. Upon Dr Lickerman's advice to devote herself to the terminally ill, she eventually finds her way out of her depressive state. Similarly, she also reconciles her feelings of guilt at not having done enough for him while he was still alive. It is never too late to uncover your purpose. Some people discover their purpose while young, as did Beethoven who was destined for musical greatness from a tender young age. Others mature into their purpose, like Gandhi who at the age of sixty-one led a nation-wide protest against British imposed taxes. His stance against authority continued well into his late seventies prior to his assassination in 1948 at the age of seventy-eight.

Equally, there are a number of people who have been called to their purpose, while others accidentally uncover their purpose when they least expect it. There is no prevailing formula for finding your purpose. The key factor lies in the commitment to action and perseverance. As you work towards creating a remarkable future, finding your purpose may become the single biggest undertaking you will achieve. Connecting with a deeper sense of purpose will enhance your life in innumerable ways, least of which includes striving to live in accordance with your highest self. One must remain open to inner guidance – by learning to trust intuition as opposed to the mindless chatter which occupies the mind. Seek the advice of those who have traversed the path before you by studying the steps they took to uncover their purpose.

As well-intentioned as family members endeavour to be, soliciting their advice contrary to your views may work against you. Family members who have not pursued their dreams may dissuade you from following yours. They'll recite any number of reasons why earning an honest living is safe, since it delivers food on the table and puts money in the bank. Yet playing it safe does not award you a prize when you are not conforming to your highest values. A quote by Oliver Wendell Holmes reminds us that time is constantly against us, as the opening story to this article makes reference to, *"Many people die with their music still in them. Too often it is because they are always getting ready to live. Before they know it time runs out."*

Do not be lured into the premise that *someday* you will take action, since that day may never come. I am drawn to the admonition by the late Randy Pausch whose famous YouTube video and same-titled book *The Last Lecture*, captivated the hearts and minds of millions of people the world over. This timely quote from Randy Pausch's book underlines the battle to overcome time through inspired action, *"I think the only advice I can give you on how to live your life well is, first off, remember... it's not the things we do in life that we regret on our deathbed, it is the things we do not."*

So how does purpose fit in with rewriting a new life script you may ask? Well how will you know what your life script will be if you have not discovered your purpose? Many people sail aimlessly through life impervious to their life choices until a crisis or awakening ensues. They remain trapped and helpless by their choices, believing there is no other way – they feel trapped and helpless. You have choices and they speak volumes of what you are capable of achieving in life. Yet to realise your potential and awaken to your magnificence, you must connect with a deeper sense of self in order to arouse that potential. Your purpose is your soul's call to life. When you are in harmony and in alignment with your purpose, doors and opportunities open in the most unassuming way. The following affirmation is testament to the ease and simplicity in which life reveals herself through you, *"In an easy and relaxed manner. In a healthy and positive way, I allow life to flow through me."* Therefore, suspend your ego in order to hear the silent call of your soul communicate through you.

How will you know you are in alignment and connected to your soul's purpose? A wonderful feeling of warmth, reassurance and expansive energy permeates through you when you are living your purpose. Personally, I feel the energy reside within my heart centre when I am caught in the flow of the experience connected to my purpose. I am overwhelmed with emotion and feelings of euphoria. There is no human emotion which comes close to the feeling one experiences when connected to your soul as you live and breathe your purpose. It becomes a part of your nature.

Consider the following points for finding and connecting with your purpose. I feel they are worthy of mention to help guide you.

Discover your passion – What do you deeply connect with? What brings you joy when pursuing this interest? Is it playing a musical instrument, painting, writing, teaching or something else? Perhaps you are still discovering your passion. That is great. Take your time. You see, as we mature we start living our lives practically. Consider stepping out of the practical world and think back to how you were during your childhood. What did you like the most? What did you spend your time doing? Think about the events of your childhood. Can those passions be converted into career choices? When you are working at a 9 - 5 job, your mind tends to be orientated on the wall clock. But what is it that makes you lose track of time? Do you enjoy the creative pursuits? Or maybe being of service to others brings you joy? What makes you forget about the clock? There are many things that bring out the child in you. Focus and exceed yourself in those areas. If art or drawing is your passion, make it your resolve to become an experienced artist - maybe not professionally, but it should fulfill your dreams.

Whom do you idolise? Do you have a role model? Emulate or model their behaviour. Whatever they do might be your passion. Understand what draws you towards them so much. Maybe they are social workers and you just want to be more involved with social services and help people. If your role model is a singer, maybe you always wanted to be a singer but never pursued that calling fearing you might fail or might not be good enough compared to others. Even if you do not want to make it your profession, it is always a good idea to not let that passion die. If you are a singer, sing a little each day. Remember that your passion is a gift from the universe. Your gift back is to share it with others.

Your life's theme – If I asked you to write a short narrative on your life in the form of a play or motion picture, how would it look? What is the plot? Who are the main characters, apart from you? What is the underlying theme? i.e. overcoming obstacles, learning to love, self-acceptance, discovering talents. These questions allow you to discover the mystery of your life. Looking back over your life, you discover the uniqueness which shapes your purpose. Use those experiences as a guide to formulate your life purpose. In many ways the book *The Alchemist* is such a tale in which Santiago, the shepherd boy, goes in search of his treasure, only to find it was at home all along. Your treasure is within your reach and contained within your life's experiences. Life leaves us clues as to our purpose, although we feel we may not be able to fill those shoes or it is not the vision we had planned for our life. Coincidentally my life's themes have involved overcoming illness in order to awaken to my greatest potential and in doing so, it is no surprise I spend my days writing and speaking about this very topic. Your purpose is staring at you – it's right beneath your nose, do not complicate it.

Moments that have shaped your life – Do you recall graduating from college or high school? Your first romantic relationship? Being awarded a prize for achievement or service? It may be the complete opposite; losing a loved one to a life threatening illness, reconnecting with your paternal or maternal parent, since they were absent when you were growing up? Write down these major moments and reflect on what they mean to you. I am certain if you were raised by a single parent or a loved one died at a young age; relationships form an integral part of your life. Reflecting on this may lead you to tears. Perhaps your purpose is a meaningful relationship, through deep love. Enriching life moments offer us a doorway into ourselves on a deeper level. They reveal our authentic self and true character. Your life's experiences are narratives told by you – use those lessons from the experiences to shape your destiny and purpose. Do not discount them as mere experiences you would rather forget, since they hold vital clues to your future path. Deepak Chopra's quote is a poignant reminder of the need to trust that your purpose will be revealed to you, through your willingness to receive it, *"You find your path not by thinking, feeling or doing but by surrendering. This reveals the impulses of spirit beneath the mask of ego."*

If you are living your purpose at present, may you continue to shine your talent and genius on the world. If you are one of many who are still discovering their purpose, fear not; for every mistake or dead-end is drawing you closer to your pot of gold. There are no mistakes in this purposeful universe – even a mistake or wrong turn has been perfectly orchestrated to allow you to be exactly where you need to be.

Give Meaning to Your Life

Consequently, as you give meaning to your life, you create an empowering life script insofar as what motivates you and inspires you. For many people, motivation stems from their external reality as they manage their life from the outside-in. However, in order to create a compelling future, we cannot rely on motivation alone to drive us forward – there must be something powerful which we connect with to create a deeper sense of fulfilment. Therefore, how do we find meaning in our life? What are the qualities that determine meaning? In order to create meaning in one's life, we must become more in order to summon the purpose and meaning we seek. By becoming more, we strive to become a better version of ourselves whilst improving upon the qualities we currently hold.

There have been countless stories throughout history depicted by those who sought to create meaning through confrontational circumstances. In many instances meaning was ascribed not to the experience, rather toward overcoming the experience, which shaped the person they became, once they moved through the challenges. One need only look to Victor Frankl, the Austrian psychiatrist held captive by the Germans during the war. Frankl's book, as mentioned earlier, *Man's Search for Meaning* contains a pivotal quote which underscores man's willingness to assign meaning to his life, *"Striving to find meaning in one's life is the primary motivational force in man."* Therefore, once we attribute meaning to our life, a powerful sense of purpose is aroused since we have given value to something greater than us. It is no surprise those who have been in the service of others, such as; Mahatma Gandhi and Mother Teresa, similarly created their own meaning by connecting their purpose to something greater than themselves.

So how can you create meaning in your life so as to strive to live a remarkable future? Firstly simplify life. Determine what is important to you and live those values and principles by embodying them at a deeper level. What is important to you means eliminating anything that is not conducive to your highest potential. It means a focused resolution to become the greatest version of yourself and in doing so, the meaning you search for becomes an extension of the value that you impart to others. It is no secret that many of the people throughout history have created meaning when they have been in the service of others. Being of service does not mean donating your time to charities or becoming a volunteer. Being of service denotes creating value towards humanity, which did not previously exist. It entails bringing your talents, genius and gifts to humanity.

Secondly, eliminate that which is not conducive to your potential. Eliminate destructive people, thoughts, beliefs, material possessions and that which stands in the way of revealing your inner wisdom. As you eliminate these aspects from your life, your mind becomes orientated toward that which is of value to you. All your efforts and inner resources are subsequently devoted towards that pursuit. For example; if you are a poet or a writer and constantly caught up in relationship or financial dramas, being embroiled in such circumstances affects your emotional life by restricting the flow of creative potential. Disposing of that which limits your potential frees your mental and emotional energy so as to focus your attention toward delivering value to your work.

Thirdly, create a new set of beliefs, values and principles by which to live by. Test these values regularly – challenge them by updating them as you find new ways. As you explore your horizons by becoming a greater version of yourself, you learn more, grow more. In doing so, you give more of yourself by adding value and service to others' lives. Do not get the impression that to be of service to others you must impact millions of people. Being of service on a smaller scale, closer to your geographic region, is one way of enriching the lives of others. Teachers are of service to others through their willingness to harness young people's potential. The young eventually mature into adults who impart their genius and gifts onto the world. So how do you create enriching values and beliefs to live by?

In a previous chapter I asked you to reflect on the themes and experiences which shaped your life. Use these events and lessons gained from the experiences to create a set of values and beliefs from which to live.

Finally, in order to give meaning to your life, you must develop a greater sense of purpose other than yourself to live for. Without discounting the value an employee brings to an organisation, a person employed in a job they loathe, simply to receive a salary at the end of each month, do not add meaning to their lives. There are countless people in toxic work environments showing up to work to derive a wage – it is these same people who look forward to a four-week vacation each year while similarly dissatisfied with the state of their lives. I invite you to extend yourself beyond the checking-in and checking-out of a job which does not serve your potential. You possess a powerful potential which stirs within you – arise that potential while discovering more about yourself in the process. As mentioned earlier, some people never have a chance to discover their potential before they die with their song within them. Refuse to go to your deathbed not having explored your potential. Seek to be a wet sponge, wrung out and used up so that when you die, you will have explored every morsel of your talent and genius. Refuse to give up or rest on your laurels until you have created the meaning you wish to express in the world.

Assigning meaning to your life heralds an understanding of your place within the universe. It ties your self-worth to a greater plan orchestrated beyond your understanding. Richard J. Leider wrote in his book The Power of Purpose, *"The question is not what is the meaning of life, but who are we bringing to life? And the answer must be chosen by each of us every day in our own way, because a meaningful life always begins from within, from our choices."* It is no wonder that those who lead meaningful lives have tied their meaning to being inspired. In my previous book, *The Power to Navigate Life* I outlined a formula in a chapter titled, **Be Inspired**. I proposed that living an inspired life is connected to your purpose, born out of love and passion.

Purpose + Love + Passion = **Inspiration**

Live an Inspired Life

Consider the following narrative depicting how inspiration presents itself in one person's life. Crafting a new life script means connecting with inspiration at a deeper level, like the following fictional character.

Every morning after a cup of coffee while catching up on the daily news, John retreats to his studio, a small space situated at the rear of his house. This has been John's ritual for as long as he can remember. As the hours pass, John is completely consumed by painting. It is not until evening draws near that he realises he has been painting for ten hours with only a break here and there. Now in his late fifties, John has been painting since his early twenties and has managed to carve out a successful career. His artwork is regularly featured in corporate foyers across the country, not to mention at regular art exhibits and private buyers who flock to his work. John represents one of many artists who are inspired and, more importantly, not afraid to put in the dedicated hours to create masterpieces. Inspiration is a call from the soul to express itself through you. Inspiration is not only confined to the arts, it may express itself in various forms. You may be inspired if you are a stay-at-home mother tending to your family. Inspiration is not defined by WHAT you do, rather it is defined by the **state of being** one experiences when in this state.

Inspiration is the expression of the creative mind of the universe flowing through you – and it is not exclusive to artists. If you yearn for direction, inspiration may be beckoning. How can you tell the difference between inspiration and happiness, since they often share similarities? Inspiration is characterised by a deep sense of joy and fulfilment. When you are inspired and pursuing your passion, time stands still. You are oblivious to your surroundings. Those who are inspired find meaning and purpose in their work, which we identified earlier as key attributes. They view their purpose as a calling rather than a job or career. They function from a higher frequency, allowing the source of their inspiration to flow unimpeded through every cell of their body. Happiness on the other hand is a fleeting experience. You may be happy one moment but not the next – happiness is a short lived state. We might conclude that happiness is ephemeral, bound by the constraints of one's inner wellbeing and external reality.

Consider the following points to cultivate inspiration in your daily life. It is worth reiterating that you need not be an artist, musician, dancer, etc. to connect with inspiration. Cooking and sharing a delicious meal with your loved one at the end of a long day may be regarded as an act of inspiration, since it is a calling from the heart.

Discover your passion and connect with purpose: What are you most passionate about? What stirs your soul and leaves you daydreaming throughout the day? Those who find passion and purpose report an overwhelming sense of satisfaction, joy and bliss throughout their life. Their spirit is alive. Not only does time stand still, one feels the expression of their soul come alive. Happiness becomes an extension of universal intelligence, which serves as the conduit of this life-force flowing through you.

Identify with thoughts that foster inspiration: It seems nowadays, life has become a constant battle for survival. Amid the backdrop, inspiration takes a backseat as the mind is caught up in *survival mode,* rather than being *inspired.* Weed out thoughts which do not resonate with your deepest self or allows inspiration to make its way into your life. Let go of disempowering thoughts of lack or limitation since they can stifle inspiration. As you distance yourself from such thoughts, you create a space around them rather than becoming invested in every thought. Drop those thoughts which no longer hold a place in your mind and replace them with empowering ones. It will not happen overnight, yet with persistence and compassion you can entertain thoughts which serve your highest good.

Develop a purposeful vision: A purposeful vision is one that is connected to your why. Why do you want what you want? What is your underlying motivation in all your actions? A purposeful vision is the pursuit of that which resonates with your deepest self. To others it may seem trivial or a waste of time. To you, it is an opportunity to connect with your purposeful self – pursue it with determination. Your determination to succeed will be governed by how strong your why is. If you have a strong enough why, success becomes an extension of your efforts. Your why is your call to action. It is your internal reference and guidepost leading you towards your purpose-filled vision. In the film *The Lord of The Rings*, Gandalf reminds us to connect with a deeper sense of meaning and purpose by posing one simple question, *"All we have to decide is what to do with the time given to us."*

Inspired people can't wait to wake up in the morning: Inspired people do not sleep in. You might be surprised to learn that inspired people are often insomniacs. Many of them ruminate in a positive way about their passion, even while asleep. They live in the present moment. They practice infinite patience, since they are not bound by the constraints of tomorrow or yesterday. Inspired people do things which buck the trends considered normal by society. You may be surprised to learn a number of inspired people harness inspiration by making time for brief power naps throughout their day in which to recharge. Not only does a twenty to thirty minute nap serve to lower stress, it improves cognitive function and stimulates right brain neural activity. They constantly nurture and feed their emotional life by creating opportunities to express their inspiration.

Inspiration is an act of Flow: The concept of Flow known as *Optimal Experience,* is a way to connect deeply with a pursuit or passion and was developed by the Hungarian psychology professor, Mihály Csíkszentmihályi. Flow is the inner state one experiences when consumed by passion. Therefore, a violinist may be said to be in Flow during a live performance on stage. Inspiration is heightened when one is in Flow since they are connected with higher brain regions, notably the right hemisphere. The good news is that inspiration crosses over into other areas of your life as you become open to it. Inspiration loves to be called upon, so the more space you make for it, the more readily it is available

What ignites your passion? What allows you to feel completely engaged in the moment? Being absorbed in your favourite hobby, sport or past-time naturally comes to mind. You might recite the countless hours spent in pursuit of that interest and the feelings associated with it. In his commencement speech at Stanford University in 2005, the late Steve Jobs imparted to graduates the following wisdom, *"...and the only way to do great work is to love what you do. If you haven't found it yet, keep looking. Don't settle."* Whilst he was alluding to one's career, we can adapt this statement to reflect other aspects of our lives where our passions run deep. Do not limit yourself when exploring ways to connect with inspiration. In order to create new life, you must be willing to live your life from a higher perspective. This perspective encapsulates your new thoughts, ideas, emotions and level of consciousness. Inspiration is one such area which invites higher levels of consciousness to permeate throughout your life.

Step into Your Dreams

In a similar vein, whilst following your dreams may seem elusive to many, it is one of the most fulfilling quests you may ever undertake. Ask any person who has traded their career to follow an endless dream and they'll advise you they have not worked a moment in pursuit of their passion. Yet for many, chasing one's dream may be filled with fear and trepidation. The fear of the unknown is stifling to some. For others, placing their trust in a universe that rarely interacts with them can be soul-destroying. Since an early age, children are encouraged to follow their dreams, the advice eschewed by parents and teachers alike. Whilst the guidance is well intentioned, there is an apparent shift which takes place by middle school. High school counsellors are quick to recommend one pursue a course of study streamed in maths, science, arts or humanities. Given university entrance scores depend largely on final year high school grades, it makes sense to shift the focus from dreams to grades.

Therefore, as teenagers approach their formidable years of educational life, the nostalgia of pursuing dreams shifts towards a fixed reality. Almost overnight the notion of *following your bliss*, as the American mythologist Joseph Campbell so eloquently conveyed, is extinguished. Nevertheless, irrespective if you are starting out or following a meticulous plan to pursue your dreams, doing so is an invitation to write a new life script. You may have been previously stuck in a job which you disliked in your former life, while looking forward to the day you will finally turn your back on that career. Creating a new life script entails claiming your power in the knowledge that your dream is your call to reconstruct the past by creating a compelling future. A small caveat – do not be soothed into believing your dreams is lined with the romanticism Hollywood films have espoused. Henry David Thoreau, the American author and poet, wrote in his masterpiece book *Walden, "If you have built castles in the air, your work need not be lost; that is where they should be. Now put the foundations under them."* He was of course referring to the hard work required to bring your dreams to fruition.

Your dreams emanate from your soul since they represent the creative potential of universal wisdom coursing through you. Your dreams are a call to pursue that which you love, yet similarly serve others. You have been awarded unique gifts that help you paint your life's canvas. Such gifts may be tied to your talents, skills and genius. Listen to the call of your soul by harnessing your potential – develop them and polish them until they are brilliant so that even the blind are aware of them. On your journey toward the realisation of your dreams, you will meet with challenges, obstacles and roadblocks. Be ready for them. They are essential to your experience of realising your potential. Summon your inner wisdom when you feel lost or disconnected with your purpose. That feeling within advising you to continue forward is an inner resolve; an inner conviction which says **it can be done.** Your task is to draw on that inner state as you encounter challenges. Let me advise you, those obstacles will appear as sure as the sun rises each day. Meet the challenge head on. Despite not knowing how to navigate your way ahead – trust the process will be made known to you once you commit to the path.

In many ways people are too quick to give up on their dreams since they believe them to be impossible to achieve and beyond their reach. Pursuing dreams are hard – dare I say challenging at the best of times, with little signs of success along the way. However, almost overnight everything can fall into place if the timing is right. Often, with persistent effort, your dreams may miraculously turn into reality when you least expect it. Be vigilant and tenacious in your pursuit of them. Develop a powerful inner conviction and sense of purpose when the going gets tough – this can only be harnessed through defeat. It is through repeated setbacks that one's inner strength and conviction is realised. There is something undeniable about the human spirit – our strength and resolve is borne out of character. The need to improve gives rise to the search for meaning and purpose. Challenges and obstacles should not discourage you from pursuing your dreams. The setbacks and pitfalls lining your path to success are meant to serve as invitations to find a way through. In many ways people are impatient and want success now, devoid of the hard work and vital lessons gained along the way. Psychologists refer to developing emotional resilience, which is reflected in the setback and challenges the journey offers. However, acquiring emotional intelligence seeks to define one's capacity to defer gratification. We crave assurance that there will be money and food on the table, instead of constantly struggling to make ends meet. Yet it is the struggle which forms our personal character, as we draw closer to realising not only our potential, our dreams at the same time.

Similarly, your focus should be towards acquiring small steps, rather than wanting to arrive sooner. At times you may feel powerless to navigate ahead – do not be concerned with the next steps, for they will be made known to you at the appropriate time. Each step and process unfolds in good time, to reveal the path ahead. Rush the process and you risk leapfrogging into unchartered territory. Given your intentions are well meaning, through sustained daily effort, success may be imminent. The most overused advice delivered nowadays is that one enjoys the journey rather than focus on the prize. Ask anyone who has achieved a level of success and they will inform you those times of uncertainty remain etched in their minds. Life will never be the same once you have achieved success. There is no turning back – savour the people you meet, the time to yourself, the struggles, the laughter and most importantly enjoy yourself while pursuing that which you love. These are moments in time which can never be relived.

Excuses hold you back from pursuing your dreams since they keep you safe, although remaining safe stifle one's progress. Those who achieve big things, dream big. They fail often and are not afraid to keep trying. Do not compromise your dreams by keeping them at arm's distance because it feels safe. Safe does not yield the results you deserve. Safety is akin to carrying around an emotional blanket in the event your dreams do not arrive as you wish. Oftentimes people make excuses when their dreams fail to materialise as they imagined, citing any number of excuses. Yet the underlying factor is a fear of failure or worse still, a fear of success. To step into your dreams, one must have an undeniable burning desire. Establish deep roots for your dreams to grow and nurture them daily. Create a powerful why which we examined in a previous chapter. Connect with purpose and intention. Demand the best of yourself and invariably the universe will greet you with a suitable reward. Doors begin to open in strange and mysterious ways when you are aligned with purpose.

We must also be willing to embrace failure as part of the journey towards our dreams. Failure is not inclined to halt your progress or disempower you from realising your vision. It serves as a way to help you get it right the next time so you move closer to your dreams. I suggest failing often, fail fast, and mostly importantly **learn** from your failures. If you are not failing often, you are not taking sufficient risks towards your dreams. Therefore, it is vital that you reframe failure by viewing them as a guidepost toward success. It is worth reinforcing that it is an opportunity to improve. Besides, who ever said life was going to be easy pursuing your dreams? I am yet to come across a single biography of those who had an easy path towards realising their dreams. Every successful person who has achieved notable success did so with hard work, persistence and an undeniable tenacity and will to succeed despite the odds. They had an unrelenting desire and commitment to create something – a strong vision they wished to bring to life – I urge you to find that same desire within. Similarly you may realise that making sacrifices are inevitable along the journey. It was Oprah Winfrey who said, *"You can have it all, just not all at once."* Sacrifices do not equate to deprivation. You need not work around the clock to succeed, and besides that will only lead to burn-out. You must be willing to give up aspects of life that will inevitably yield long-term results. Never sacrifice family life, since you can rarely recover broken relationships. In fact, as you make compromises, your family life should be the last aspect traded for success. Certainly, make adjustments along the way where required. Sometimes life will present you with unexpected detours – take them. Trust and have faith that you need to acquire an essential skill for your dream to thrive. Steve Jobs credits taking a calligraphy class at college which later helped him create fonts for Apple computers. There are no mistakes.

CHAPTER 10

Take Control of Your Life

Take Control of Your Life

"A sign of wisdom and maturity is when you come to terms with the realization that your decisions cause your rewards and consequences. You are responsible for your life, and your ultimate success depends on the choices you make." — Denis Waitley

Whilst we are not always in control of the currents of life, we have the power to direct our reaction to what unfolds by greeting life's changes with openness. While we have limited control over certain aspects of life, by casting the arrow, as it were, we surrender to the forces of life to direct the unfolding of events – that is where the arrow will land. This simple metaphor reminds us of our role as co-creators of our life's events, although in a number of ways we ultimately surrender control to a greater power, which takes care of the details. You might call it fate, destiny, pre-determinism or a higher power.

In order to accept control of your life, it is essential that you inhabit your body by aligning with your mental and emotional self. Be present by owning your thoughts and emotions – do not dismiss them as an inconsequential facet of your being. You are the director and producer of your life's narrative. When I discuss inhabiting your body, I refer to a state of ownership and connection of your mind and body. I also refer to being present and grounded in the moment, not at the mercy of your past or future thoughts or similarly any runaway emotions which vie for your attention. When you inhabit your body you do not require stimulants to create an ideal *physical state*. Being in your body means honouring your natural gene expression as nature intended. You are in command of your thoughts and emotions. You do not blame others for the way they treat you, since you assume ownership of co-creating every experience in your life. It is said we **coach** others how to treat us. If you frequently play the victim saying, *"He/she is responsible for the way I act or feel"* you deprive yourself of your potential to enjoy life since you are at the mercy of others. You yield power to others and lose sight of your self-worth. As you surrender your power, others will use it according to their level of awareness. That is, you binding yourself to others by assuming control of the relationship rather than being a balanced union.

In many ways it is fundamental that you release past mistakes and regrets so as not to carry them into the future. The present is your gateway to the future. We touched on this in Part I of the book. What occurred in the past resides merely as nothing more than a memory. To replay the past by inviting it into the present moment is not conducive to living a remarkable life. You are held captive by your thoughts and emotions when you habitually replay past memories. Thoughts and emotions create a kaleidoscope of chemical reactions within your body that influence your genetic destiny. Releasing the past entails making peace with the past and learning from the wisdom gained from your experiences. It invites you to bring love to the process by letting go of hurt or anger or any other untoward emotional states. The lesson from your experience served its part in your soul's journey toward personal growth. The present moment contains the seed of opportunity, which invites you into the future. If you re-live the past through toxic thoughts, you deny the future from making its way into your life, since your frame of reference is stuck in the past. Your mind cannot dwell in two places at the same time. It cannot live with past regrets and strive toward future happiness. Liberate yourself of one and subsequently another door opens to transport you into your future. The mental and emotional energy required to live in the past is lost on opportunities that are better served for your future.

Stepping out of your way represents dropping the resistance brought to each moment. Through your resistance to life, you block the goodness unveiling itself through you. Many struggle with the concept of universal intelligence working in their favour, since they focus purely on the negative aspects of life's events. Your perception creates and colours your reality. What you focus and dwell upon becomes your focal point; irrespective of whether it is good or bad. As you relinquish the need to control outcomes, you accept what permeates through your life as valuable lessons contained within each experience. Your lessons become the experience you are having right now. Like it or hate it, the universe brings you this experience for your personal growth and is vested in the expansion of your connection to the deepest aspect of your nature. How you respond to the experience serves as your lesson. Similarly, your lesson may not be packaged in the form you might expect. For example, if it is in your interest to learn the value of friendship, you may find yourself in opposition with a close friend with whom you do not share the same outlook. In such a way universal intelligence assumes this experience as vital to help you accept your personal power within the friendship. We may be bestowed with the opposite experience of what we expect the lesson to be. The boxing metaphor, rolling with the punches encompasses accepting what shows up in your life as a valuable lesson serves your highest growth. Wisdom has taught me that every time I refused an important life lesson, I'll be given a new one disguised in different form.

It is worth appreciating as you create a remarkable future, you expend less energy toward material possessions, people or circumstances which do not matter. If it does not feel right, let it go – follow the wisdom of your heart by feeling your way in to the experience. A quote by Dave Ramsey reminds us of the need to please others at the risk of a contracted self-worth, *"We buy things we don't need with money we don't have to impress people we don't like."* Can you identify with this quote? It involves courage to go against the crowd and stand for something different. People will influence your decisions by advising you of your inability to achieve a certain goal or dream. Do not waste time validating yourself by succumbing to this way of being. The energy required to validate yourself stems from resistance and is futile to living a compelling future. Rather, pursue that which brings you joy. Let go of material possessions and relationships that do not enhance your personal evolution so as to usher in the new. Thinking with your heart asks you to feel the world instead of think of the world. Connect with your feelings often – **feel** your way toward a fulfilling job, career, relationship, life etc. How does it feel when you consider each of these scenarios? Your feelings are accurate representations of your call to action.

Know when to back down and when to advance. Create your set of rules and abide by them. Do not subjugate yourself to other people's way of life assuming it is the accepted model or simply because others have always done it that way in the past. Be consistent in your pursuit of the truth and a way of life that serves your potential. If you desire to be the best in your chosen field, practice daily or as Malcolm Gladwell advises in *Outliers* – embrace the 10,000 hour rule while focussing on deliberate practice in order to be world class. Do not give up at the slightest hint of failure. You are frequently being tested by the powers of the universe to determine your courage, tenacity and intent. You will be presented with more challenges along the way, each time you conquer a new one.

Refuse to accept anything less than your best insofar as your heart's desire. Find a way; create a new path if none exists. Recognising when a pursuit is futile is equally important. Sometimes it may be vital to relinquish your current path in order to follow a new path. This simply means you have ventured down the path as far as it will lead you and it is now time to move in a new direction. Life may pull you away from what seems like a futile cause in order to provide you with a valuable skill to use in another area. An unexpected U-turn may pose as a blessing in disguise and does not imply that all is lost. Upon reflection and with the passing of time, we see the value of the experience. Create the life you deserve with enthusiasm – create it with unbridled passion towards the process of life. Be inspired in your pursuit of your ideal future, since motivation alone is insufficient to create a compelling and powerful dream. Motivation wanes as the going gets tough. Inspired people harness the power of infinite creativity as the source of their wisdom, often with less effort and greater reward. Create the life you dare possible. It exists on the other side of your fears, doubts and anxieties – be so bold and approach life with vigour and enthusiasm.

Step Out of Your Comfort Zone

As you assume control of life, serendipitous events begin to unfold leading you to awaken your inherent wisdom within. At this level you must be willing to step out of your comfort zone in order to greet life with passion and fervour. Here is an all too common scenario that plays out in many people's lives and illustrates how settling sometimes can shift us into a state of apathy and comfort. Life tosses you lemons – well at least that is what you suspect from where you stand. You may be sick and tired of being in rut, thinking the same thoughts. Feeling uninspired – emotionally drained and lacking direction. Do not despair in such a situation since you may simply be experiencing an internal shift.

From time to time, you may suffer periods of uncertainty, which on the surface appear as though your world is sinking. You feel helpless and unable to navigate your journey ahead. Though you cannot quite put your finger on it, something is not quite right – you know that part at least. Life seems harder and requires much more effort than usual. Everything is a chore. You are swayed into emotional turbulence at the slightest episode when things do not going according to plan. Rest assured, life is not always smooth sailing. Seeking refuge in that statement liberates us from having to push against the forces of life. Like any journey, the intention to reach one's destination is typically heralded by a goal or a plan, although you fail to anticipate the rough waters ahead. That is, you might have to sail your boat in unchartered waters in order to reach your final destination.

Life's journey is filled with boundless lessons, which we often fail to concede when embroiled in our own drama. In Paulo Coelho's book, *The Alchemist* Santiago, the young Andalusian shepherd acknowledges his trek across the world filled him with wisdom and a great deal of knowledge owing to the people he meets along the way. His journey has not been a waste of time after all, for he has gained much from his experience in search of his treasure. Contained within every effort, every step, every so called failure draws you closer to your treasure – your pot of gold. Nothing is wasted. No effort has been in vain. There is a rhythm and timing to the universe which one must abide to if he is to realise his potential. With that in mind, stepping out of your comfort zone may be paralysing to some, since there is a level of anxiety associated with uncertainty. We become accustomed to the familiar and so, rocking the boat, destabilises our equilibrium. Author Neale Donald Walsch of the acclaimed spiritual book series, *Conversations With God* said, *"Life begins at the end of your comfort zone."* Dealing with uncertainty and change can be debilitating in terms of our imposed stress, yet seemingly living a compelling future requires we step out of the familiar in order to reach new horizons.

The chart below illustrates how our comfort level is associated with our desire for change. Typically, the stronger the desire for change, the more discomfort we feel, as we move toward the unknown. Similarly, depicted in the quote by Lao Tzu is a reminder to allow the process of life to unfold without adding our drama to it, *"Life is a series of natural and spontaneous changes. Don't resist them - that only creates sorrow. Let reality be reality. Let things flow naturally forward in whatever way they like."*

Remember it is your response to life which is paramount to the level of personal growth you undertake. Most people respond favourably in ideal situations, although this does not test one's character, since most people naturally thrive in successful situations. Your response to life's uncertainties determines your level of inner growth, especially when the tides are against you. You might recall that

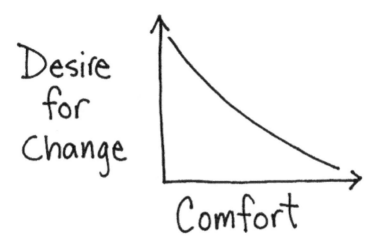

in chapter eight, I declared my fascination with the mindset of billionaires, owing to their incredible tenacity to overcome external forces. A self-made billionaire requires profound confidence to never give up, given the economic forces of life are continually against those reaching for success. There must be an inherent self-belief, an unyielding motivation and a desire to prevail. To succeed you must adopt similar qualities in your pursuit to step out of your comfort zone. Do not rest on your laurels since it is easy – remember easy is not where the fruit of your success lies. You must be willing to take risks, whether big or small and gradually move in the direction of your dreams.

It was David J. Schwartz who wrote the bestselling book, *The Magic of Thinking Big*. In his book he reminds us of the power of belief as a measure of pursuing your dreams with a powerful intensity, *"Those who believe they can move mountains, do. Those who believe they can't, cannot. Belief triggers the power to do."* Familiarity keeps you safe and oftentimes stuck and stagnant. Most people are quite content to sail through life impervious to their potential. They rather not take risks in the event life does not emerge as they hope for. Subsequently, their self-esteem is likely to take a hit and they are to perceive themselves as failures. Yet failure and self-esteem are not inextricably linked. You are not a failure because your goals fail to materialise in the way you hoped for. You may have been unsuccessful in reaching your goal, although you may be drawing closer to success each time, yet are unaware of it. It was Tony Robbins who said, *"Success leaves clues."*

Stepping out of your comfort requires you to extend your personal boundaries in order to create a fulfilling life. Successful people whom you look up to have pushed past their comfort zones in order to reach their current level of mastery. They broke through many a glass ceiling to create a new way of life and similarly paved the way for others to follow. That is the inviting aspect of pushing past your comfort zone – you serve as a guidepost for other to follow, by breaking ground in your pursuit. Yet as alluring as it might seem, to push through your comfort zone, you do not want to make it a constant quest. Integrating your experiences into your life becomes paramount, since it is defined by your learning and inner growth, which becomes the focal point of pushing past your comfort level.

Fear as Your Best Friend

Similarly whilst our aim is to move beyond our comfort zone in order to create a deeply compelling destiny, there is a hidden element which rears its ugly head that I will discuss here. Often, throughout our life's journey, our fears become overwhelming to the degree in which they stop us dead in our tracks, like a deer in the headlights. We become consumed with a crippling state of anguish, unable to navigate our way through it. At the deepest level, any fear holding you back serves to appoint the lesson vested in faith and courage. Consider how life will be five, ten or twenty years from now if you refuse to conquer your fears? Reflect on the following story depicted in the book *Influence Science and Practice*, where author Robert Cialdini shares a story capturing the transformative essence of fear. In a tribe in southern Africa, the Thonga people hold an annual initiation for young boys prior to becoming a man. A young Thonga boy must endure a series of intense physical challenges before he is admitted to adulthood.

The three-month ritual consists of six major trials: beatings, exposure to cold, thirst, eating unsavoury foods, punishment and the threat of death. As bizarre as some of these rituals sound, the young boy emerges a man and in doing so has learned to silence his inner demon – fear. Whilst the idea of spending three months subjected to mental, emotional and physical hardship might seem harsh, consider how many of these young boys become strong and powerful leaders within their tribes. This story illustrates how fear, despite the brutality of the ritual, can be channelled toward personal growth.

In civilised society, fear impairs the lives of many who buy into the notion that fear is real. It was the French philosopher René Descartes who said, *"I think therefore I am."* In other words if there are thoughts, there must be a thinker behind the thoughts. Moreover, many people unknowingly buy in to the false premise *"If I think fearful thoughts, they must be real."* You've heard it said that fear is an illusion created by the mind. A great deal of what we fear rarely comes to fruition, yet fear seems to predominate our thought landscape. Since fear is a survival instinct that alerts us to impending danger, it only becomes a threat when our thoughts become stuck in a repetitive cycle. When fear rules your life, you are at the mercy of the emotion.

How can we reframe fear to view it as friend rather than a foe? Firstly; appreciate fear as a feedback mechanism alerting you to forward progress. You are stepping out of your comfort zone and moving into uncharted territory. Rather than oppose fear, embrace it by viewing it as an opportunity to gain new insights as you advance onward. This is especially true as you embark on letting go of the past to create a compelling future. Embrace the fear by observing it as part of the process of evolving. You are stepping out of your comfort zone and naturally your mind is unaccustomed to the new stimuli. In serving to protect you, it alerts you to impeding danger, which it perceives as a threat to your wellbeing. However, the fear should be viewed as an illusion as you progress into uncharted territory. Many people view fear as a brick wall, while others see it as an opportunity to overcome. Fear is your best friend since it inspires a call to action. It advises us to avoid that which is deleterious and take affirmative action. Take for example the fear of public speaking, which is considered one of our greatest fears. The American comedian Jerry Seinfeld offers us the following comedic observation, *"According to most studies, people's number one fear is public speaking. Number two is death. Death is number two. Does that sound right? This means to the average person, if you go to a funeral, you're better off in the casket than doing the eulogy."* In this instance, fear forces us to brush up on our speaking skills through rehearsal. Rather than appearing incompetent, fear forces us to show up prepared. As we overcome fear, we not only build character and inner strength, we overcome an impediment on our path to victory. Therefore, fear becomes a great teacher, since it provides us with the experience before the lesson.

Moreover, fear reminds us to stay connected to the present moment. Given fear is a future occurrence; it allows us to reconnect back to the present moment when our minds wander into the future. We are reminded all we ever need is contained within the perfection of this moment. There is no need to worry or fear a future which seldom arrives as we hope for. Therefore, fear reminds us to let go of the incessant thoughts of an anticipated tomorrow. It must be affirmed that we cannot eliminate fear from our lives, not in the way many people believe. We can turn down the volume on fear by not becoming a slave to it. Susan Jeffers' acclaimed self-help book, *Feel the Fear and Do It Anyway* is an appropriate axiom for learning to befriend fear. When faced with the prospect of taming our fears, we are reminded that fear helps us sharpen the sword, as it were, by making better decisions in lieu of perceived danger. We must have our wits about us as we confront our fears.

Your response to fear provides a glimpse into your deeper psyche. Are you continually running away from fear or willing to face it head on? Fear is a call toward inner growth and freedom. Running away from your fears makes them grow stronger until they overwhelm you. Rather than oppose your fears, approach them with compassion and an open heart. Forgive yourself and others who may have contributed towards your fears. You might be surprised to learn that a number of our fears are passed down through generations. Wars and hatred stem from the paralysis of fear. First we fear that which we do not understand, then we ultimately go to war with it. If we dislike parts of ourselves, then this becomes a call to make peace with that aspect of our nature. You always have a choice – to make peace with fear or allow it to control your life. Hopefully I have provided you with some valid points to choose the former. Transcending fear is liberating since it frees you from the self-imposed fortress, which is the illusory mind of fear.

Let Go of Your Fear of Failure

While preserving the notion that fear is your ally, consider the following questions as we explore transforming your fear of failure. In many ways, one of the biggest impediments to living a successful life is allowing fear to dominate our life if left unexamined. Remember fear is a barometer and a feedback mechanism, offering you an opportunity to deal with underlying beliefs and emotions, which serve no place in creating a remarkable future.

What does failure represent to you?

When did you last experience failure?

What lessons (if any) did you acquire from the failure?

Failure may have various implications to a variety of people. It can cripple some, while for others, it is simply the opportunity to start afresh with a renewed approach. Where does the notion of entitlement to instantaneous success arise from? History is celebrated with those who failed miserably, yet pursued their dream with staunch determination. Oftentimes, the journey leading you toward the fulfilment of your dream may be more rewarding than the victory itself. I outlined this in an earlier chapter which explored the concept of Flow. The process may be imbued with purpose, passion and excitement and in a number of instances, more gratifying than the victory. Your dream, whilst still alluring, takes a backseat as one is completely consumed with the process. Flow is the opportunity to be at one with your quest – to be totally absorbed in the present moment.

The following analysis offers you ways in which to reframe your fear of failure. I should render a caveat at this point that fear is a trained response. Anytime we entertain fear, we reinforce its power. In order to break the cycle, one must be vigilant to habitually guard their thoughts. Defend the entrance to your mind like a fortress.

Getting to the heart of your fear allows you to trace its origin whilst understanding its primary purpose. Fear has an origin. Get to the heart of it.

Similarly, failing fast suggests that the bigger the dream, the greater the likelihood of setbacks. Failure in this context is inevitable due to the size of your purpose. Bigger dreams require additional steps, many of which lay obscured, hidden out of sight. In a number of cases, these steps are revealed once the journey is undertaken. Therefore, it is advisable when pursuing a big dream that mistakes are limited to early in the piece. Your aim is to gain valuable insights before persevering onward. Failing fast invites you to harness vital lessons from the experience and thus transform them into success further down the path. Failure is simply pointing you toward an aspect of your dream which requires attention in order to assure success. Viewed from this perspective, failure becomes a signpost pointing you in the right direction, rather than a negative event. Perhaps there needs to be additional steps undertaken in order to reach your final objective.

Personally, I like to remind myself that failure is not permanent. It is edging me closer toward my desired outcome as long as I remain vigilant and determined to learn from the setbacks along the way. It has the potential to become permanent if you fail to learn from your mistakes. Failure is a transitory process since it continues to make itself known until you have mastered the lessons to forge ahead. I urge you to read an inspiring book about overcoming failure called *Delivering Happiness*, in which Tony Hseih founder of online footwear retailer Zappos overcame numerous failures to build one of the largest online footwear businesses in the world. In recent times the company was sold to Amazon for close to $1 billion dollars. Equally, history is marked with people who were consumed by fear yet persisted in the face of it. The death of fear is imminent when we take bold action. It was Dr Orison Swett Marden, American author and founder of *Success* magazine who said, "*Most of our obstacles would melt away if, instead of cowering before them, we should make up our minds to walk boldly through them.*"

Likewise, remaining grounded in the present allows us to detach ourselves from fear becoming a future phenomenon. We fear the unknown since we have an expectation of how life should unfold. When life does not develop according to plan, we suffer. Your body is always in the present moment, so it stands to reason that your mind occupies the same space in time. Do not be consumed by future worries or concerns. Do not waste valuable resources imagining a future which never arrives as you expect. When you love what you do, fear of failure becomes an illusion, since you are no longer attached to outcomes. The future always arrives at precisely the right time when you choose to practice infinite patience. All your needs are met in the moment of time called now, so there is never a need to rush the process.

Overcoming Self Doubt

We have covered ground in this chapter to outline ways in which to take control of your life, while defining the impediments that impose on your personal growth. It would be remiss of me to not mention the silent killer to many a man's dream – self-doubt. It is an all too common experience – the silent, yet incessant self-doubt which inhabits your mind, combined with the stream of destructive thoughts that accompany it. The voice does its best to command your attention, while reminding you of your inherent weakness. The ceaseless inner dialogue knows no boundaries until it completely overwhelms you. In that very moment you surrender to the self-doubt, knowing it has taken hold of you once more. Welcome to the intimidating inner critic and modest detractor determined to undermine your success. Despite your best intentions to overpower the crippling self-talk, it seems futile since self-doubt sustains its hold on you. Why won't it leave you alone you often wonder?

You cannot remove doubt any more than trying to eliminate negative thoughts. Doubts are woven into our psyche during childhood as we learned to integrate into our surroundings. Similarly, what begins as the voice of reason echoed through loved ones, soon becomes the doubtful inner critic given the passage of time. We are notorious for falsifying inaccurate tales about ourselves. Doubt is one such story that is often repeated through adulthood. Whilst it is healthy to entertain doubt from time to time, being at the mercy of the debilitating thought is not conducive toward living a remarkable future.

In a similar vein, doubt can become self-deprecating while wreaking havoc with your personal confidence if left unchecked. It is worth repeating that self-doubt requires self-examination if it prevents you from living an enriching life. It is apparent that a growing number of people are quite content to shy away from honouring their highest potential. They conceal their emotions deep within, hoping they will miraculously vanish, and no, these same people are not confined to the male class either. Unfortunately, with the passage of time, the buried emotions may resurface in the form of illness, destructive relationships, addiction to substances or untoward behaviour, etc. In his book Spontaneous Evolution, author Bruce Lipton states that 95% of our behaviour is controlled by our subconscious mind. In many ways our behaviour is reflected in the blind decisions we make every day without a moment's consideration. Reflect on how much of your daily life's decisions are automated, that are devoid of conscious intent?

In another example, author Michael S. Gazzaniga further illuminates this point in his book, *Who's In Charge: Free Will and The Science of The Brain.* As a neuroscientist investigating split brain personality, he offers the following observation about the choices we make, *"That you are so proud of is a story woven together by your interpreter module to account for as much of your behaviour as it can incorporate and it denies or rationalizes the rest."* A great deal of articles, books and resources have been written about self-doubt in recent times. Most apply the term *conquering doubt* rather dismissively, likening it to overcoming a setback. It may benefit you to reframe doubt as an integrated aspect of your nature – since it resides within your shadow self. You need not deny aspects of yourself, for that which you resist continues to persist. Overcoming self-doubt requires taking affirmative action while being attentive to the inner critic – that is, you choose to take action in spite of the doubt.

In a documentary highlighting the sport of accelerated free falling, the jumper was asked by a reporter if he entertained fear prior to his jumps. He reassured the reporter that fear was present during every jump and served to remind him of the inherent dangers associated with the sport. He managed fear by choosing to turn down the volume on it so as not to be overwhelmed. This leads us to examine the purpose of self-doubt. Does it serve to mask a repressed aspect of oneself? Take a moment to consider the spectrum of doubt inherent in your life. What tools or resources do you frequently call upon to navigate self-doubt when it emerges? It should be stated that doubt is merely a self-imposed speed bump in your life's journey toward fulfilling your remarkable future. As you know speed bumps are intended to slow you down, not halt your progress.

If self-doubt is wreaking havoc in your life, reconnect with your compelling purpose, which we outlined in chapter one of Part II. Your vision of your future cannot be obscured by self-doubt, since if given enough emotional energy it has the power to kill your dreams even before they have begun. Similarly, attributing self-blame in relation to past failures leads to more of the same destructive thoughts embedding itself into your psyche. Instead, choose affirmative action with respect to your goals and attend to your doubts with self-compassion. It is your responsibility to reconcile them in a peaceful manner free of guilt. Remember, your journey towards a compelling future is lined with many detours. Embrace your challenges with attentiveness and enthusiasm. You have heard it said that it isn't the dream that fuels our desire. It is the journey towards whom we become that ignites our passion and sustains us in attaining inner victory.

CHAPTER 11

Step Into Your Own Power

"Strength does not come from physical capacity. It comes from an indomitable will."
— *Mahatma Gandhi*

You may have settled for sitting on the side-lines instead of getting involved in the game of life with passion, purpose, and power. It is no secret those who lead a fulfilling life have the power to create their own circumstances, owing to their enthusiasm and passion. Have you allowed life's circumstances or setbacks to frustrate you or influence your mood? You would be one of many who react to their environment by internalising their external reality. As testament to internalising our experience of the world through thought and emotions, author Jamie Smart writes in his book titled *Clarity: Clear Mind, Better Performance, Bigger Results*, *"You're feeling your thinking, not what you're thinking about..."* Consider the question, is there something holding you back from stepping into your power? If there is one thing that excites me more than anything it is having the privilege of encouraging and motivating men and women to recognise and step into the magnitude of power that resides within them. It is persuading them to open their eyes to the ways in which they have allowed mental illusions and lack of clarity to hold them back. It is awakening within them a fervent desire to run toward their dreams with great expectancy and joy.

Your mind is possibly churning with thoughts, which is not a bad thing, but if a lot of those thoughts are negative, it will affect your beliefs and actions. I am sure you can relate to occasionally lying in bed at night trying to go to sleep while your mind is running wild with anxious thoughts. You want to sleep, but you ruminate about any number of situations hoping to resolve them in your mind. It makes for a very tired person the next day I can assure you, since that was the person I was prior to meditating and bringing peace to my thoughts. It is certainly worth investing the time to learn how to silence your thoughts and let your heart lead the way, since your heart knows everything that you really want and need for a happy life. Besides, have you noticed that most of the things we worry about never actually happen? I am certainly not announcing anything new here, yet only in hindsight do we realise how much energy is lost in mindless thinking. In chapter six, Lessons on Forgiveness I mentioned that we entertain anywhere between 70,000 – 80,000 thoughts a day. Most of those thoughts are repetitive in nature. It makes sense that we abandon this way of thinking in place of seeking clarity through our thoughts as author Jamie Smart reminds us.

As a brief aside, mindful meditation is a wonderful practice used to quieten your thoughts. In this practice, you take some time to sit still, take a few deep breaths, relax your entire body, and focus on your inhalation and exhalation. As you focus on your breathing, many of your thoughts cease and you experience inner peace. Occasionally a floating thought or emotion will enter your mind. This is alright. Simply acknowledging the thought or emotion and letting it float away is enough to bring peacefulness to your thoughts. This simple practice teaches you to manage your thoughts and emotional state, rather than being at the mercy of your runaway thoughts.

In order to step into your powerful self, learn to face and embrace your feelings and emotions rather than become a victim to their erratic nature. We know that situations in life often arise which are not optimal; there may even be trying circumstances that evoke negative feelings. What you do with these feelings is vitally important as it relates to moving forward or staying stuck internally. Many people do not like to feel pain, so they stuff their pain as they encounter it or try to numb it with addictions, constant activity, etc. The effects of these ineffectual coping skills drains vital energy over time, perhaps leading to an emotional breakdown at some point in the not too distant future. Through mindful meditation you learn to embrace and process emotions. It is alright to temporarily feel the intensity of the emotions, whether it is sadness, grief, anger, rage or otherwise, but then allow them passage. They may have arisen in order to teach you a lesson or finally deal with emotions that you have stuffed for years. Accept what surfaces by allowing it to reveal itself through you. Like a full moon on a cloudy night, trust that behind the clouds lies the brightest light that cannot be diminished.

The ability to embrace your emotions and attend to them will help you to become more powerful in a number of ways. You become more secure and confident, as well as happier and more peaceful, since you are processing the emotion rather than ignoring it. Young men are taught at a very early age by well-meaning fathers not to show their feelings since it is deemed to be effeminate and not in keeping with their masculinity. Yet it is these same men who are prone to emotional breakdowns or mid-life crisis since they have suppressed their emotions so much so that they erupt. There is general consensus among happiness experts who assert the more fully you embrace your negative feelings, the more you can experience the positive feelings as well. So rather than sailing through life feeling a little happy, you can realistically learn to embrace and honour your negative emotions, which allow you to experience abundant and authentic joy, which is after all your default state of being.

One needs only to look to young children to see how delightful and playful they feel most of the time. It is only through growing societal and personal pressure that we internalise a state of internal stress and lose sight of our playful nature. As you honour your feelings, you express self-love by reclaiming your wholeness. You do not deny any part of you, which allows you to step into your amazing power that has resided in you all along. By stepping into your own power, you claim the inherent power that resides within us all. It is there waiting to be claimed, but first you must let go of the conditioned beliefs and false judgements you have accumulated over the years that obscure your powerful self.

Seek the Truth

In keeping with stepping into your own power as a means to create a planned future filled with promise and meaning, I would like you to consider over the coming paragraphs what pursuing the truth encapsulates for you. It is no secret that power and truth are synonymous, since one cannot exist without the other. As you assert your inner power, you live an authentic life which is bestowed in the truth of your being. To live your truth gives relevance to honouring your highest principled virtue, bound by the essence of your highest self. The higher self is the quintessential aspect of who you are – it is the embodiment of your spiritual nature, unbound by human weaknesses. Living your truth must come to represent that which is true for you alone and unhindered by outside influences. In previous chapters we examined the unconscious programmes and beliefs that obscure the truth from revealing itself through you. Your truth is the essence of your spiritual nature – that is, once the mental facade has been transformed, the truth gives way to the light of your being. In doing so, you overcome emotional impediments that may stifle your growth. The truth is represented by the emergence of the authentic self, which is the soul's true essence.

Noted for his acclaimed work as an internationally renowned psychiatrist, consciousness researcher and spiritual lecturer, the late Sir David R. Hawkins, M.D., Ph.D., wrote many compelling books, his most notable being *Power vs*

Force. He teaches us of the essence of truth being akin to letting go of the falsehood of our thinking, *"Like the sun, the inner Self is always shining, but because of negative clouds, we do not experience it. It is not necessary to program oneself with the truth; it is only necessary to remove that which is false...It is only the removal of the negative that is necessary-the willingness to let go of the habits of negative thinking. The removal of the obstacles to the experiencing of this will result in an increasing sense of aliveness and a joy of one's own existence."*

Seeking the truth entails living life according to your highest principles and values. You are pulled by your empowering beliefs, values and ideals, which you honour deeply, for these principles allow you to express your authentic nature. As testament to this, the following list encapsulates my truths, which I have refined over the years. How do you know you are living your truth? Well, problems begin to give way to solutions in the easiest manner. Life has a vast richness, which is not bound by external forces. You are drawn to revealing the highest version of yourself, whilst knowing through personal growth you are constantly letting go of that which no longer serves your potential.

- I respect and honour myself.

- I invite others to allow their authentic wisdom to emerge.

- I treasure the knowledge and wisdom within me.

- I respect and honour those I come into contact with.

- I withhold judgment about others, for it is not my place to judge.

- I honour my purpose by being of service to others.

- I live in accordance with my highest truth by connecting with my inner wisdom.

- I express myself according to my highest moral values.

- I do not hold on to disempowering mental or emotional states,

- I am the conduit and expression of life's infinite creative potential.

Your truth serves as your roadmap, it is your guiding force – your light and beacon to navigate your way ahead. Whilst we make daily choices that guide our life's path, living in accordance with our truth is the highest choice we make. What you accept as your truth becomes your destiny. Your truth influences your beliefs, thus impelling your actions. I truly believe at a deeper level we are striving to do the best we can given the resources available to us at the time.

Your level of awareness shapes your life, for as you grow in awareness the veil, which obscures reality, is lifted to reveal the truth. There may be times when we unwittingly offend others through our choices and actions. If we abide by our truth, we trust that we cannot please everyone and therefore as long as we act morally and dutifully, we are following our deepest wisdom. I am not suggesting our truth harm or offend others. As we live our truth, it should unite others toward a common goal, the expression of humanity through oneness.

History has been marked with those who have earnestly pursued their truth by opposing popular held beliefs and societal norms. Mahatma Ghandi and Martin Luther King firmly believed in causes greater than themselves and were willing to take a stand for their truth, i.e. equality among men. Consider what principles you hold close to your heart? What moral values do you honour? How does honouring your truth serve you? How do know they serve you? When did you first encounter your truths and was there ever a time when they were challenged? A number of questions to consider, yet if we fail to live by that which we hold value to, how can we expect others to interact with us when we have no measure of influence on our own life? These questions must be asked if we seek to discover a fundamental blueprint for the attainment of happiness and a fulfilling life.

In many ways, today's failed marriages serve to highlight the discontinuity men and women hold toward a nostalgic view of marriage. Their truth does not represent their own rather that of a collective society (media, friends, family, colleagues etc.), which asserts that you remain unfulfilled until you have married and had children. Unfortunately a number of men and women buy into this false mirage by marrying incompatible partners to please their family, or even worse, owing to the fear they may remain single and very much alone. Regretfully, divorce highlights the inevitability of both parties to naturally grow out of their union as they realise their truths no longer serve them – it was in fact someone else's truth they were living. Whilst I am using marriage as an illustration, we could relate it to your career, finances or key relationships. The value of the message is to realise your truth before someone else imposes theirs onto you. It may take months, years or even decades. Besides what is the rush? It is better to discover your own truth through trial and error than to live other people's truths. In his book *Unapologetically You*, behavioural science academic and author Steve Maraboli advises us of the importance of this position, *"Live your truth. Express your love. Share your enthusiasm. Take action towards your dreams. Walk your talk. Dance and sing to your music. Embrace your blessings. Make today worth remembering."*

Freedom is attained within the deepest realisation that your destiny rests in your hands. In many ways Mahatma Ghandi and Martin Luther King were prepared to die for their truth by standing for something greater and more compelling than principles alone. Whilst one need not die for his truth since we have become liberated from oppressive societal ideology, realising your truth represents the highest act of authenticity one can attain. Beauty and honour is attained by those who stand for something – that is, someone who strongly believes in a purpose, a vision or an ideal for which they lose sight of the trivial aspects of life. You need not strive to be a Ghandi – yet as you seek to represent your truth, you guide others to do the same by creating a path for others to follow.

It was the greatest intellectual of this century, Albert Einstein who wrote, *"Man should look for what is, and not for what he thinks should be."* Therefore, I invite you to discover the truth of what is, rather than what should be. Reveal your authentic self by becoming attuned to the essence of your being. Your true nature is not concerned with what you do for a living, how much money you have amassed, how many followers you have on Twitter, nor how many Facebook friends you have accrued. Your true nature seeks to connect you to your deepest beliefs by allowing them to serve you and similarly others in the unfolding of your deepest wisdom. You seek the truth through the significance of the questions you put forth. In time, life reveals itself through you as you become the question; seeking the truth.

Live Passionately

As you step into your own power, life invites you to live completely while immersed in passion. In many ways in seeking the truth by living to our deepest values, living passionately is a call to summon enthusiasm towards life. You will agree that life is certainly a journey full of hills, valleys, bumpy roads and sometimes smooth roads. Sometimes it is predictable and sometimes it is not. There may be periods where everything seems to be going well and other times when it seems like you are a magnet for negative distractions. No one is impervious to the torrents of life. We all experience the trials and misfortunes at various times, however what everyone does have is the opportunity to adopt a positive perspective no matter what they encounter. Let's face it, tough times show up, people will let you down; you will experience loss, failures and setbacks. You can choose to focus on the negative aspects or you can choose to orientate your focus on the positive aspects. You have a choice in every moment as to how you respond to life – the cards you are dealt do not determine your destiny, rather the way in which you play the game.

Attitude is paramount as it relates to whether you live a life full of passion and purpose or one of regret and resentment. You may have encountered people who have been through countless ordeals and repeated setbacks and yet still emerged with an optimistic attitude, especially towards others by bringing blessings to those in need. They chose to learn valuable life lessons through their ordeals by embracing a positive perspective regardless of the circumstances. How do you live a life full of passion and purpose irrespective of when life does not eventuate as planned? The way in which you manage your emotions determines the level of passion you bring to your life's experiences. We noted in a previous chapter that emotions are simply energy in motion, therefore if your emotions are primarily unconstructive, you are bound by those emotional states that keep you stuck. You are at the mercy of your negative emotions, rather than seeing them as a guidepost pointing you to empowering emotions instead. Conversely, if your emotions are optimistic, you are choosing to live a life full of passion, joy, peace, and purpose.

Embrace life with all your senses.

To live a passionate life, learn to embrace your senses. That is, do not hold back your emotions, rather embrace them, experience them, process them and let them go. This is a healthy way to handle emotions since emotions want to move through the body. It has been shown that toxic emotions have the potential to move through the body and wreak havoc in a short amount of time. As mentioned before, the work of brain scientist Jill Bolte Taylor suggests that the average lifespan of an emotion to move through the nervous system is one and a half minutes. Knowing this releases the burden that we need to carry our emotional attachments longer than need be. We rarely take the time to examine our emotions until they have wreaked havoc throughout our life. Without the risk of creating a war among the sexes, women prefer to talk about their emotions while men subscribe to the adage *out of sight, out of mind.* Perhaps men inadvertently choose sports as a way to release pent-up emotions without conscious motivation. In many ways, like physical health, our mental and emotional wellbeing is equally important to living a passionate life.

Daniel Goleman's much acclaimed book, *Emotional Intelligence* gave rise to the term EQ (Emotional Intelligence). He states that your ability to manage your emotions is a strong precursor to long term wellbeing and success. Numerous social and psychological studies conducted over the years have measured children's EQ's in order to predict future success. In a number of these studies, supervising psychologists followed up with the children years later throughout their teenage and adult lives. They noted those who displayed higher EQ as children were more likely to have a positive and optimistic outlook as adults. Therefore, living passionately may arise as early as childhood.

Pursue that which you love

Whilst you may not entirely appreciate every aspect of your life, you certainly can pursue that which deeply resonates with your deepest being. Pursue that which you love is the underlying message echoed by the Rumi quote, *"Everyone has been made for some particular work, and the desire for that work has been put in every heart."* Life becomes demanding; attending to work, children, family responsibilities and managing stress, so it is vital to make time to engage in activities you love. The feelings that arise as you engage in these activities will refresh and invigorate your spirit and enable you to live a life full of passion and vitality. What do you love to do? Stop right now and consider what brings you joy and passion. Make a commitment to pursue those things more frequently without getting caught up in the day to day rituals of managing life. Be adventurous and bold by rediscovering the joy of doing old things again. Do not simply resign yourself to restrictions or impositions which restrict your ability to interact with life. Remember passion flows where attention goes.

Bring your *whole self* into each experience.

Did you realise that you only know the *tip of the iceberg* about most people? What this means is that people choose to reveal their good side most of the time. As the majority of an iceberg is submerged under water, the less revealing side of people is buried as well. No one likes to reveal their whole self, since it is embarrassing to admit you have a darker side, known as the shadow-self. To live a passionate life means to bring your whole self into each experience; the good, the bad, and the ugly. I am not advocating acting out character defects, rather I am suggesting it is perfectly acceptable to reveal your authentic self as we touched on in the previous chapter which is devoid of ulterior motives or hidden agendas. Those involved in a newly formed intimate relationship, often discover their partner mirrors their darker side. In essence, they bring to the surface issues you have not brought out into the open or aspects of one's shadow-self, which remains repressed or unconscious. Owning your issues by working through them allows you to seek inner freedom by liberating yourself from destructive emotional states. A life of passion is found on the other side of integrating your negative state into the wholeness of your being.

Release expectations

Whilst planning and goal setting certainly has its rewards, be aware that often, despite meticulous planning, life does not go according to plan. Therefore, allow room for detours and pit stops on your life's journey. Many times, the most rewarding life experiences show up when you least expect them. As you release expectations as to how life should unfold, you will naturally feel more freedom and passion towards life, since you are no longer bound by tense emotions towards future expectations. Viewed from this perspective, expectations are premeditated resentments. Certainly while it is perfectly normal to have goals and plans of action, I invite you not to be so rigid with them that you risk your personal, mental and emotional wellbeing.

Relax. Release. Allow

Make room for the new

Just as computer software needs to be upgraded every so often, be willing to upgrade yourself too, by making room for the new. It is said that nature abhors a vacuum and will fill anything left in its place with some new. Change is inevitable and a natural process of life if your desire is to step in to your magnificence. Release the tired, old programs, perspectives, beliefs and outdated programmes which no longer serve your potential and inner growth. You will have noticed this has been the theme circulating throughout this book. Make way for the new, the fresh and vital expansive energy and you will undoubtedly notice passion invites its way into your life with equal fervour. Given these changes are made gradually over time, your perspective and life's circumstances will unfold in the timeliest manner. You are entitled to live a life of passion and purpose. Focus on these key points for as brief as thirty days and witness your life change within a month. Rest assured you can reinvent yourself in the timeliest manner to find enjoyment in life more palpable.

Reclaim Your Life

As you step into your power, there is a powerful exchange to tackle life with renewed enthusiasm and passion. Consider the following questions. Do you feel as though your life is one endless drama after another? Are you constantly wishing your problems would simply dissolve into nothingness? As a contrast, recall a moment in time when you were on vacation, without a care in the world. It's as though time stood still and all your mental and emotional concerns simply vanished while you were on holiday. I have spoken with countless people over the years who vowed their life would be different once they returned from vacation. They would create more time to unwind, relax and not take life so seriously. Invariably, given their well-meaning intentions, the haste of life takes hold and they find themselves back to the same old routine.

There is a way to reclaim your life while not allowing your defeats and struggles to define who you are. I often discuss this topic with a friend who likes to lament on his most recent toils. It is as though he jumps from one drama to another, while endlessly protesting there must be a better way. My friend touched on a point in a discussion, which fixed itself in my mind. As one who has struggled financially over the years, he was looking for a way to leave his meaningless job. He sought to run a business that would allow him more free time to pursue other interests, yet most importantly, a job which offered mental and emotional satisfaction. He refused to be defined by his strive for a better life any longer. He felt when and if success arrived, he would be incapable of appreciating it since he had become preoccupied with worry and tension for most of his adult life, that in some way he had become a victim to the pain. The notion of living a purposeful life was now an elusive dream.

Have you ever experienced a similar situation?

Reclaiming your life is not defined by an external change in circumstances, rather it requires a resetting of your internal compass. The decision to create a new blueprint to live a remarkable life must come from a deep desire to change for the better. The Freudian psychological principle known as the pain–pleasure principle states that humans have an inner drive toward seeking pleasure or conversely running away from pain. You either attract opportunities that serve your highest potential or get stuck in a painful cycle of undesired outcomes. The downfall of the pain cycle is that you learn to model the behaviour of mice within a lab experiment administering electric shock. In order to reclaim your life, take ownership of your thoughts, choices and actions. We are solely responsible for steering the course of our destiny. As to which harbour your ship ventures into rests on the forces of life. Your mission is to continue progressing forward through life, despite the consequences of life.

Many success and leadership experts speak of the need to reframe failure if we are to lead a fulfilling life. I recall early in my career how debilitating failure was to my personal identity. As time passed and with a number of failures under my belt, I let go of the need to attach failure to my personal worth. In fact when I let go of failure as a negative consequence, I sought to view it as something which had very little power over me. Similarly, you may wish to view failure as an opportunity to advance closer to your dreams; not further away. Do not attach failure to self-esteem as we mentioned in previous chapters, since doing so will derail your progress. Transform your frustrations and fears into enthusiasm and passion. People who are enthusiastic and passionate are more inclined to enjoy their journey through life. In doing so, they seldom focus on the end result. If you love what you do and do what you love, the process can be more rewarding than the final result.

You will have grasped the idea to pursue that which resonates with your deepest self by this stage. Everything else is extraneous when you identify what is most important to you. Far too many people focus on superficial pursuits while neglecting the bigger picture. They believe that by undertaking everything they lay their hands on will ultimately return a favourable outcome. This may be akin to painting a masterpiece by throwing paint at a canvas, wishing it would transform itself into a Rembrandt. Most importantly, do not let life pass you by. Take life by the reigns by being in command of your choices. Whilst you have little control over the outcomes of those choices, you still have the power as to how you respond to them. I am particularly drawn to this wonderful quote by the late poet Maya Angelou, *"Life loves to be taken by the lapel and told: 'I'm with you kid. Let's go."* Reclaiming life then becomes an extension of one's inner state of being. Once you attain this state, your inner and outer worlds collide in blissful harmony. There is no striving, since everything you do becomes an extension of your inner world. An inner peace and purposeful action arises from your efforts, owing to being inspired to make life happen, rather than respond to the circumstances of life which arise.

CHAPTER 12

Find Yourself and Be That

Find Yourself and Be That

"Men go abroad to wonder at the heights of mountains, at the huge waves of the sea, at the long courses of the rivers, at the vast compass of the ocean, at the circular motions of the stars, and they pass by themselves without wondering." — St. Augustine

In the quest to discover one's potential, many people wander aimlessly, dazed by a sense of confusion. Numerous self-help books line the shelves of bookstores proclaiming the latest movement or program to heal you in thirty days. Self-help groupies seek solace in New Age wisdom only to discover what is already contained within – the source of all wisdom. Given we live in what is arguably the most prosperous period in the world's history, why have we lost our sense of self? This confusion has given rise to a popular meme now used synonymously throughout the Western world known as first world problems. Whilst I do not mean to diminish the value of self-improvement, the mere fact you are reading this book points to a desire for constant personal improvement which is commendable.

I affirm that our maladies may be attributed to straying from our life purpose; while similarly succumbing to external influences. The young are inundated with a plethora of information, fuelled by technological advances that have allowed us to stay connected, especially via social media. In many ways our connections are nothing more than empty posters on an electronic billboard, which serve to remind us we belong in some way. And yet, we have an inner longing for social acceptance. It is wired into our DNA to be a part of a tribe. The following paragraphs are what I consider to be the quintessential qualities for reconnecting with your essential self. Find yourself and be that means to connect with the essence of your being; rediscovering the core-self by living in alignment with your deepest wisdom, rather than seeking solace in an external event, person or material object.

Accepting yourself as you are involves complete acceptance of oneself by acknowledging your wholeness with all your imperfections, foibles and insecurities. You cannot disown unfavourable aspects and seek to highlight positive qualities. This might be deemed treading a fine line toward narcissism. As you accept yourself as you are, you serve to unite your disowned parts by integrating them into your wholeness. Similarly, a deeper knowledge of oneself seeks to represent the understanding that at a deeper level, you are more than your thoughts and emotions. I am not referring to knowing your likes or dislikes either. Rather it is a call to discover the true essence of your spiritual self. Who is the real you? What are your genuine motivations? What kindles your soul? What are you most passionate about? Who is this person you call the self? As we uncover our true nature, we realise all those things we have attached to our personal identity are merely labels to give us a sense of place in the world.

Moreover many people create a false sense of self in an attempt to form an image of who they think they are. Discarding the false self is a call to abandon the beliefs and thoughts of who you think you are in place of discovering a stronger sense of self. It is believed the mind creates a false persona epitomised by the ego to keep itself alive. Unfortunately, life events (tragedy or loss) may disrupt this image and suddenly one is faced with the task of re-examining their sense of self, since the illusory shadow is shattered. It should be added that distancing yourself from your thoughts will allow you to gain a clearer perspective of your true self. You are not your thoughts, you are the thinker and receiver of the thoughts in as much as a radio is not defined by the signal it transmits. You cannot argue a radio is specifically bound to an FM or AM frequency, since it transmits both frequency bands and in many ways your thoughts are the frequencies you habitually entertain. As you may know, you entertain empowering thoughts, while other times your thoughts may be less than desirable. Therefore, do not allow your thoughts to give you an impression of your real self. Thoughts come and go, yet the essence of who you are is unchanging and authentic – connect with that part of your nature. Finding yourself beneath the veil of your obscured identity is often a challenge owing to the numerous addictions we hold onto, which keep us safe and secure. Controlling addictions may extend to material things, people or situations. Addictions may also extend to habitual thoughts that occupy valuable energy in your mind and body. In essence, they disconnect you from your precious self. We have already outlined the case in previous chapters for letting go of that which does not serve you. The Buddhism aphorism invites you to drop it like a hot piece of coal.

In many ways we strive to seek validation in some manner in an attempt to feel connected and part of a tribe. We do this in order to make up for any shortfalls we experienced during childhood. Therefore, if you grew up in a household where your parents were emotionally distant, you may seek validation from others in order to feel better about yourself. Whilst there is nothing wrong with the feeling of positive emotions, doing so at the risk of relying on others to fulfil your happiness is fraught with long term unhappiness, since your inner wellbeing is dictated by external sources, rather than your own. Therefore, let go of the need to prove yourself to others or become a people pleaser. You do not require validation from others to prove your worthiness; even from loved ones. No one or nothing can offer you the authentication you long for, other than yourself. True validation comes from the core of your being. Your core self is a wellspring of positive feelings, which are available to be called upon. In some ways we may believe our core self has been obscured by life's tragedies, hence we lose sight of connecting with it. It becomes a thick fog as we are unable to see the forest for the trees.

Similarly, as you seek to connect with your core self, it is vital to find time for regular silence. By finding time for regular silence, you allow yourself to connect with your true nature. You would agree that our thoughts occupy much of our attention at the best of times. Stressful and anxious thoughts conceal the core-self from revealing itself. It is the shy, introverted inner child whose voice is drowned out by the incessant, inner critic which is habitually vying for attention in your mind. Find time to be alone every now and again, particularly in nature. Spending time outdoors allows you to reconnect with your essential nature within a tranquil setting. Being outdoors harmonises both mind and body and energises the soul. You might be interested to know our cells are orientated to transmit an electrical charge, which corresponds to that of the earth. Earth's resonant frequency, which is known as Schumann resonance is, 7 – 10 cycles per second, measured in Hertz. The average reading is 7.8 hertz. This reading also correlates with that of humans and animals and allows for harmonic resonance. You will feel energized and in tune with your natural state as you spend more time in nature.

Also vital to uniting with your essential being is the need to align with your heart and mind. In my book *The Power to Navigate Life,* I titled a chapter, *Connect with Your Heart and Mind* since I believe many people unknowingly live life from the level of the mind. The problem with thinking your way through life level is that you become stuck in left brain logic, since you were taught from early age to reason the world through logic alone. As mentioned above, it has been demonstrated in experiments that the heart's electrical impulse is 40 to 60 times greater than the brain's. The heart often feels or initiates things well before the brain has time to make sense of it. Recall how your major life decisions were made through feelings and intuition? We often talk about a situation *felt right* or it was a *gut instinct*, eluding to the power of the right hemisphere to guide our choices when we learn to harness its energy. Similarly, I invite you to accept the perfection of life through the awareness that you do not have to change anything *out there*, since the root cause of your troubles is always contained within. As you tend to your inner world, your external reality harmonises with it. As the Hermetic aphorism states, *"As within, so without."*

Granted, oftentimes we may focus our attention on pleasing others at the risk of downplaying our self-worth. We have touched on this idea throughout the book. I encourage you to focus on yourself first before tending to the needs of others. I do not mean you neglect others needs by becoming self-righteous or narcissistic either. As you cultivate your own needs first, you become better suited to help others in a more powerful way. This is a basic principle of leadership whereby the leader retains the qualities he/she wishes to see in their followers. Tend to your inner world and nurture it by taking time for regular self-examination and introspection.

Being the irrational creatures that we are, we fail to see past our tragedies to realise life gives us encouragement even though it may not appear in the form we expect. Yet your time here is not meant to be a cycle of pain and suffering. It is within your power how you chose to respond to life's unfolding events. Contained within that choice are your greatest lessons if you withhold judgement on how life should develop.

To concede defeat, you award power to those unpleasant events by perpetuating the victim's role, which is an easy trap to fall into. And so, with restrained patience we remain vigilant in how we respond to life's ups and downs.

Happiness is a choice, not an unattainable goal.

You move toward happiness the moment you declare your intention to do so. Equally, we may be content, yet happiness may elude us. When happiness entails our material and emotional needs being met, we allow it to permeate our lives with unbound richness. With our basic needs fulfilled, we want nothing more than the comfort of being present within our own body. Even unwanted thoughts fuelled with fear or anxieties are powerless over us since they are transitory states.

Your obligation is to abide by something deeper if you wish to live the life you deserve. Stand for something which conveys control and a reason to attend to the day. We receive what we ask of life. What we claim equates to our self-worth. Our self-worth is in direct proportion to the sum of our life's experiences. You cannot demand more if you are undeserving at some level. If you have issues with receiving, this is likely to show in how much life affords you. However, if your beliefs coincide with what you deserve, that becomes your reference point.

Unresolved childhood wounds are often related to unworthiness issues that perpetuate through maturity. Perhaps your main caregiver convinced you of your unworthiness and you have held onto this all this time. In his book, *The Mind Body Code*, author Dr Mario Martinez affirms this point stating, "*You were never robbed of your power or your worthiness; you inadvertently disowned them.*"

For that reason, avoid responding to subjective thoughts to what is lacking. Do not concede to disempowering thoughts based on an internal script. With enough energy, these learned beliefs sooner or later transform into negative states. Your reality is formed by aligning with your deepest values, not by reciting worn-out childhood inner dialogues. This is not who you are, any more than choosing to associate with your childhood toys. Reality is reflected in your thoughts, desires and beliefs on what you deserve and are willing to accept. "Because if the decisions you make about where you invest your blood, sweat, and tears are not consistent with the person you aspire to be, you'll never become that person," states Clayton M. Christensen in his book, *How Will You Measure Your Life?*

Be bold through your willingness to commit to your dreams. Don't be pushed by life's failures since they often redirect you to a better-suited destination if you allow the journey to unfold.

Be moved by your passion and your heart's desires.

There is discussion these days on the merit of visualising a purposeful future. Whilst much of the advice comes from well-intentioned life coaches, the guidance invites you to call on your imagination to bring reality to life. *You have to believe it before you see it* maintains the biblical saying. To embrace the life we deserve, we step into our greatness, not cower from it. You have nothing to fear other than fear itself, which holds you captive by playing small.

Marianne Williamson reminds us, "Our deepest fear is not that we are inadequate. Our deepest fear is that we are powerful beyond measure." Just like a double-edged sword, if we shy away from our magnificence, it has the potential to impair our growth if we fail to use those gifts. I enjoy Steven Pressfield's view, "A child has no trouble believing the unbelievable, nor does the genius or the madman. It's only you and I, with our big brains and our tiny hearts, who doubt and overthink and hesitate."

Be present and alive in each moment instead of floundering in the past or focussing on an imaginary future. Many people prevent a promising future from arriving due to negative thoughts and a belief they are undeserving of goodness. To create the life you deserve, take inspired action and move out of your comfort zone. "Life happens at the end of your comfort zone," declares Neale Donald Walsch.

In honouring this intent, author David J. Schwartz acknowledges this belief in *The Magic of Thinking Big*, "Believe it can be done. When you believe something can be done, really believe, your mind will find the ways to do it. Believing a solution paves the way to a solution." For in striving, we attain inner freedom and as the Buddhist teacher Pema Chodron says, "No matter what the size, colour, or shape is, the point is still to lean toward the discomfort of life and see it clearly rather than to protect ourselves from it."

Stop Running on Autopilot

Here is a key statistic I'd like you to consider as we explore the idea of unconscious actions versus conscious will in the coming paragraphs. Far too many people navigate through life unaware of how their thoughts influence their behaviour. It is as though they are asleep at the wheel, while their life hurtles recklessly out of control. Almost 90% of our daily activities are habitual in nature. You wake up, shower, brush your teeth, eat breakfast, catch transport, walk and drive or ride to work/school without so much as given a second thought to those decisions. Your subconscious mind becomes so adept at handling such daily actions, it has been suggested by the late Dr Candace Pert, an internationally recognised pharmacologist, that the body is the subconscious mind. Interestingly, your body handles all this without hesitation of the slightest conscious thought. If I asked you to solve a complex problem or learn a new dance move, you would engage your conscious mind, while fundamental to learning the new task, that is prior to the task becoming an unconscious habit.

The point I wish to highlight is that we engage with life oblivious to how our unconscious thoughts and behaviours drive most of our daily actions. Falling into the trap of running on autopilot leads you to unconsciously carry out actions that have been imprinted into your subconscious mind without conscious awareness. Unfortunately this triggers your mind to **react** to situations instead, as your mind searches its data bank for historical references in order to make sense of the present moment. To illustrate the point, assume you had an argument with your sibling relating to a subtle matter. Your sibling over-reacts and directs hurtful insults at you, which triggers an emotional cascade of retaliation. The situation is further escalated by additional spiteful responses traded between you, before one of you storms out of the room in anger. Family members have a knack for activating your pain response as it relates to your emotional disposition. The truth lies in knowing that your reactions stem from the programmed beliefs and thoughts stored in your unconscious mind.

When we are unconscious to our actions, we **react** instead of **interact** to situations. For example; some years ago my colleague and I were conducting a health seminar in the faculty of a well-known university. We were discussing the benefits of drinking good quality artesian water in place of tap water, relating it to the benefits of one's long term health. A member of the audience took it upon herself to verbally attack us, stating there was no scientific evidence to support our statements. Aside from there being a plethora of scientific evidence to support why artesian water has a higher mineral content versus tap water, this person **reacted** to our statements, rather than **interacted** with us. She could have used the situation to foster dialogue between us and other members of the audience in order to present counter arguments. This would have created a healthy forum to discuss the topic rather than become embroiled in a heated exchange of words. Following the lecture, we approached the audience member as we were both eager to know more about her strongly held beliefs. We discovered she was raised on a farm and drank tap water from an early age since that was the only source of water available. She saw nothing wrong with consuming tap water, sighting herself as testament that long term exposure to tap water showed no deleterious results. Besides appearing unhealthy, we saw no reason to challenge her on the issue, other than to concede she was neither wrong nor right in her position.

This person reacted to something that challenged her beliefs, rather than saw it as an opportunity to foster creative dialogue between us. We had ignited her pain body as Eckhart Tolle calls it, by directly challenging her long held beliefs. As we challenged her belief system, her initial **reaction** was to launch into an attack instead of reconciling whether the belief was still relevant. Unfortunately, many people remain stuck on autopilot, never challenging the legitimacy of their beliefs and thoughts. I wish to raise within you the capacity to test your beliefs when they are challenged. Use it as an opportunity to test the validity of the belief and the basis for personal growth, rather than see it as a personal attack. You might be pleased to gain wonderful insights, which contest your long held beliefs. After all, it is not about being right or wrong – it conveys your obligation to seek happiness and self-empowerment in the long run.

As a belief or idea is challenged, the tendency is to wage a war in retaliation while not considering if the belief is valid. Nowadays, as I conduct workshops, I usually prompt participants by advising them that some of the concepts I present will challenge their long held beliefs, which may conflict with theirs. I suggest rather than attack the principles, especially if they are new to them, reflect on them by noticing any inner resistance that arises. I instruct them to conduct their due diligence by testing the ideas and thoughts before discounting them as inaccurate, wrong or outdated. In order for inner growth to occur, we must be aware, awake and receptive to new information which challenges our long held beliefs. Being challenged is never easy, since the inner critic wants to be right. Life is never intended to be a game of who is right or wrong. It was the American psychologist Gerald Jampolsky who said, *"You can be right or you can be happy."* Many of your current beliefs were formed during an impressionable period of your life, i.e. childhood, when you were in a subconscious learning stage. Furthermore, those long held beliefs were impressed upon your by loved ones and authority figures, in which you took it upon yourself to assume they were imparting factual wisdom. In many ways we are not wholly responsible for our acquired beliefs as children, although we are responsible for our actions and the subsequent thoughts and beliefs we entertain as adults.

On the next occasion you are in a disagreement with someone, stop for a moment prior to reacting and consider whether you are acting out a learned childhood programme or whether your words and actions are distinctively yours. It takes a great deal of awareness and introspection to acknowledge we have inadvertently adopted inaccurate thoughts and beliefs of others, while continuing to habitually play them out like broken records. Ask yourself that question - do I want to be right or do I want to be happy? Physiologically speaking, every time you oppose something or someone, you activate your fight or flight nervous system, which is reactive in nature, instead of interactive. I invite you to suspend your long held beliefs by repeatedly questioning them as they arise. Ultimately your exchanges with others should emanate from a position of interaction, rather than reaction. Let us remove the outdated notion of winning and losing as it relates to our connections with others. As Stephen Covey offered in his best selling book, *The 7 Habits of Highly Effective People*, one of the three values of Interdependence is striving for win - win in every encounter.

Waiting For the Perfect Moment?

Seemingly, in our quest to discover the essential qualities of our nature, many people seem content to wait for the perfect timing to go after theirs dreams and goals. The problem with this way of thinking is that it sets us up for disappointment, stagnation and failure. There is never a perfect time or day for anything. The universe consists of moving energy, so you are either moving by creating positive momentum, or you are sitting idle in stagnation. The choice is yours. If you are currently in a career or a relationship that you tolerate, but do not appreciate, you allow external factors to control you – subsequently your hopes of a better life may be dwindling due to your inattentiveness. If you are unhappy, it might it be a good time to do something about it? Or perhaps you have tried to change things to no avail. If that is the case, it is time to try a new approach.

You deserve a happy life with a matching career and relationships you enjoy that allow you to flourish – everyone does for that matter. If you have settled in areas of your life due to other people's expectations or popular culture's conditioned hype, it is time to take a stand and declare your willingness to seize the day. It is time to get clear on that which you desire and create action steps to propel you forward in that direction. I have a number of friends who are quite happy with a satisfactory job, little money and without an intimate relationship. Similarly, I also have friends who are fulfilled with a great career, plenty of money and a fulfilling relationship. They have tapped into the power of being happy regardless of their external conditions. They have learned that having an attitude of happiness and gratitude now, as opposed to someday is far more rewarding mentally and physically. They are not "waiting" for the perfect moment or situation before they allow happiness to consume them.

Most people desire a happy life and seek 'material' possessions or 'people' to feel happy, yet the root cause of their problem arises since happiness is not found in these pursuits; it emanates from within each person. It requires cultivating a path of happiness throughout life. It requires a season to slow down, smell the roses as it were, to contemplate life, face your pain, ask yourself the hard questions and challenge yourself. These have been the predominant lessons espoused throughout this book. I assure you a happy life is available to you. Perhaps you begrudgingly offer the polite form of reply, "I'm fine" when asked how you are, but really underneath the tough exterior, lies a despondent person in search of something more.

Yearning for a better life without willing to do something different is akin to being stuck on a merry-go-round, wishing the ride would accommodate you by stopping so you can step off. Oftentimes what is needed is a leap of faith literally speaking, to jump off the ride while it is still moving in order to attain the life you seek. It will not be found whilst you are spinning around in a dazed confusion. You must be willing to travel a road you have not travelled before in order to live the life you desire. We must change our thinking by stepping out of our conditioned thoughts, in order to transform our external circumstances.

I believe every person has the capacity to create a sustainable and fulfilling life once they reconcile their outdated thinking, which casts doubt over their life. Personally, I have had periods in my life where I was not completely happy – we all have. It would be remiss of me to believe that life was anything but smooth sailing, devoid of challenges and obstacles. It was not that I did not want to be happy; I did not know how to be at the time. I sought refuge in external conditions, since I bought into the illusion that the source of my happiness was contained in some external event, beyond my inner being. What I did know was how to keep pressing forward no matter what. I believed deep within, I could discover joy since the source of my happiness was not to be found "out there." Albeit, it did not arrive in the way I expected of course. Furthermore, it might not show up for you in the way you expect it, yet there is a fountain of happiness that lies within you. As you acknowledge it, you will find yourself connected to that source increasingly more – even if there is little change in your external situation. Happiness then becomes a habit as we orientate our focus by discovering delight in the smallest circumstances in life.

Surrender to Life. Live Life on her terms. Do not spend energy trying to swim against the tide. Go with the Flow. This means being flexible in your thinking. Life is extremely efficient. As you move two steps forward and one step back, realise there are no mistakes. That one step back you took may transpire to become your greatest gift in that it provides the knowledge and experience needed to fulfil your dreams. Pursue your dreams but do not be rigid in *how* you achieve success. Rather than resist what appears to be a dead end, embrace it as a blessed detour. Allow life to open doors and show you ways to achieve your dreams that never occurred to you. Surrender is not giving up, apathy and resignation are. It is part of the process to let go and trust in the universal wisdom of life. It is a state of allowing. Your ability to persist is not possible without your ability to allow. Continue to follow your heart. Believe in yourself and your dreams. Keep the faith. Anything is possible and miracles happen every day, oftentimes in the smallest way that we mistake them for bigger ones. Trust that dreams are not meant to be reached in a straightforward fashion. Some of the world's greatest discoveries and inventions were the result of divine 'mistakes. Progress is often made via a zig zag toward your goal. The universe is aligned for the attainment of your purpose and passion. We are meant to enjoy the journey, not wallow in misery since fortune favours the brave.

Moreover, stop waiting for the perfect moment to feel happy or accomplished. Take it upon yourself to make your happiness a priority. Make a declaration to your partner, your friends and family that you are going to change aspects of your life with the first thing being your perspective. You are going to stop striving to fulfil other people's expectations. You are going to discover who you are and reconnect with a joy that is bubbling within you waiting to be released. This moment is the perfect time to acknowledge your success, your happiness and your fulfilled dreams. You need not continue to wait for a certain event or situation to happen in order to find happiness and wellbeing. Life is what you make of it, so be proactive in making your dreams come true.

Develop a Powerful Presence

Pursuing your dreams equipped with a powerful intention and sense of purpose, while inviting, requires that we cultivate a call from within ourselves to activate that desire. The power of presence ignites our capacity to create a remarkable future by transforming that intention into future action. So what is this elusive thing called presence which people desire? I am frequently asked in seminars how people can cultivate more presence in their lives. I would have thought inhabiting your body was enough to foster presence. Firstly, let us define presence and examine why it is paramount for connecting with the authentic self. Consider the last time you attended a social gathering and met someone who exuded a mysterious quality. It may have been a distinctly attractive quality, perhaps a distinguished grace or a peaceful nature which drew you towards them. It may have been an elusive aspect which you were unable to quantify or it was merely that they seemed comfortable in their own skin and aware of their surroundings. They might have moved about the room as if floating on thin air, while exuding an unmistakable allure.

People who have presence have an inner radiance, since they are comfortable and content within themselves. They seldom walk or move in haste. Their gestures are timed and controlled, as if rehearsed. They rarely seek approval from others, yet it is others who seek approval from them. I have met numerous people who have personified these characteristics. Upon reflection they were the most genuine and grounded people I recall meeting. Others may incorrectly assert that it is all an act, although I am loath to buy into that argument given the congruity of maintaining such an "act." So how does one create presence? Why would you want presence anyway? And how does it serve you? Maintaining presence is the outward reflection of your inner world. It is the frequency you transmit, while advising others of your inner contentment – that is you are in charge of your inner domain. You are the master and architect of your destiny.

You might be aware that human beings fall into one of two categories relating to their personal characteristics; leaders or followers. If you are a leader you are fortunate enough to inspire and lead others toward revealing their uniqueness. If you are a follower, you are fortunate to being the recipient of such leadership and acquiring a number of the leadership qualities bestowed by formidable leaders. Let us make the distinction clear that being a follower does not imply being a sheep, devoid of thought to create one's own circumstances. Over the years I have looked up to and modelled my life on a number of esteemed leaders. All of them possessed unique qualities which I sought to incorporate into my personality and thus become inspired by. Psychologists suggest when you recognise a quality in another person you admire, you already possess that quality within yourself. Therefore, presence is distinguished by an unknown quality within you which seeks outward expression.

The following points relate to creating powerful presence in your life. Allow me to render a caveat by stating that it takes time and patience to create sound presence. You cannot rush the process any more than nurturing a growing child. You simply cannot wake up one day and be blessed with more presence. Presence is acquired, much like water filling a bath tub – recall that water always finds its own level.

Know thyself, grow thyself.

As you discover the essence of your spiritual nature, you simultaneously learn more about your capabilities. You reveal your hidden talents, as well as your imperfections; your genius and magnificence. For example, if you are inherently shy, cultivating presence may be slightly more challenging than being an extrovert. There are seldom great leaders who are shy. Granted they may possess introverted qualities at times, though their predominant qualities are extroverted in nature. Identifying with your shyness might invoke a commitment to working on developing your inner leader by allowing your light to shine. I am certainly not advocating that shy people are less socially developed. I am suggesting that shyness and leadership may not be conducive qualities if you seek to cultivate presence. As someone who regularly speaks before audiences, I experience shyness when I meet new people within a personal setting. I am far more relaxed these days and allow myself to feel at ease with the person I am communicating with. This has required a great deal of commitment from my part to step out of my comfort zone, since I have become accustomed to being in a quiet setting, spending my days writing.

Presence occurs within the moment.

Presence occurs as you are engaged within the present moment. You do not attend a social gathering and turn on presence – it cannot be manufactured or imposed on others. There are numerous actors, models and singers who have the ability to turn it on and off, given their years of training and experience. Once they are away from the spotlight, they quietly retreat into silence to recharge their batteries. You cannot be expected to be engaging all the time – those that are may feel depleted mentally, emotionally and physically once they retreat into a quieter setting. You cannot erect a facade by staging presence. A useful analogy might suggest that a light house serves to guide ships into safe harbour by shining its light out on to the sea. Seek to become that beckon of light for others and naturally they will be drawn to the light of your presence. It follows as you are open and receptive to engaging in the present moment. The key to cultivating presence is to be awake to each moment. It requires that you become present in your body and not stuck in past thinking nor worrying about an anticipated future. Gradually as you remove fear and anxiety from your life, this will enable you to see opportunities present themselves. If you are consumed or paralysed by fear, your mind is conditioned to seek it out and in doing so, this becomes your focal point. The true essence of living in the moment is that you are no longer a victim to your past or a slave to the future.

Harness self-awareness and inner wisdom.

When I talk about harnessing self-awareness and inner wisdom I refer to accessing your inner guide or your inner teacher. Recall a situation where you intuitively identified with an inner voice communicating with you or recognised a feeling summoning you to take action. I am not suggesting hearing voices either, rather the quiet whisper echoing from within. It speaks so silently that it feels like a fleeting gust of wind. If you dismiss it by drowning it out with thought, it can disappear as quickly as it reveals itself. You may have experienced moments of inspired action in the past without any prior knowledge of the situation – that is you acted intuitively. Perhaps you discovered yourself in a random place, meeting someone unknown and immediately connected with them. These are situations where you accessed your inner guide. It is your inner wisdom which knows no bounds and limitations; yet has the answers to all your questions.

As you learn to work with your inner wisdom, you access presence and unite with spirit, which is waiting to be revealed through you. Try it out from time to time by invoking it on personal matters in your life. In many ways like learning to ride a bike, you become a better cyclist by developing sound bike handling skills, which are attained through trial and error. In a similar way, the more you become adept at accessing your inner wisdom, the more others will see the beauty emanating from your soul. You become the lighthouse others are attracted to. Allow these words to find meaning in your life by incorporating them into your daily life. Learn and build on them through patience, trial and error. Do not be surprised if you make mistakes. Be kind to yourself since you are learning, growing and evolving. Remember there is no such thing as failure in life; only the opportunity to improve.

CHAPTER 13

Reveal Your Inner Wisdom

Unlimited Power

"You are one thing only. You are a Divine Being. An all-powerful Creator. You are a Deity in jeans and a t-shirt, and within you dwells the infinite wisdom of the ages and the sacred creative force of All that is, will be and ever was." — Anthon St. Maarten

In the previous chapter I outlined a number of key points to help you unearth the essential qualities of your inner being. I stated that in following your bliss and staying grounded in the present moment, you bring more of yourself into your life's experiences. That is you let go of limiting beliefs and disempowering emotions. This could be because you may not be able to recall the past within the present moment. In this chapter I will summarise how you can reveal your inner wisdom through various means, all serving to connect you to a powerful future. As you step into your future and claim it with purpose, synchronous events begin to align to help steer your path toward a future filled with promise.

Before we continue our journey throughout this chapter, I want you to appreciate that you have more power than you realise. More genius than you can imagine. More wisdom and knowledge that you can ever access. These are not patronising statements to seduce you into a false belief. You possess unlimited power, although accessing that power is the basis to the upcoming paragraphs. When we learn to let go of the false belief that we are lacking or inadequate in some way; in that very moment, we arouse our potential.

We established in previous chapters, that who you are today is a result of your acquired programs, beliefs, thoughts and ideas about the world. Unless you examine if your present circumstances are serving you, you may remain stuck and inhibited. One has only look at mainstream culture to see the effects of the media and marketing hype has on our society. We are drawn into a fictitious way of life at the expense of our sanity and hard-earned dollars.

We are conditioned to be like everyone else. We attempt to stand out by decorating our external shell, hoping to be noticed as being *different* to others in some way. Yet we entertain the same thoughts and live the same lives as millions of other people, while longing for a better way. Contemplate this for a moment – when did you last entertain an "original" thought? In his book *Do the Work*, author Steven Pressfield realised it wasn't until he was thirty years old that he pondered an original thought. Every thought prior to that period was a result of conditioned beliefs, attitudes and thoughts derived from society.

Your thoughts, beliefs, ideas, perceptions etc. are not yours, since you acquired these ideals from others from your childhood years and made them your own. Over the years you may have substantiated them by finding evidence in your external reality to prove them so. Yet every time you find evidence in your external reality, those beliefs are reinforced via your neural network.

Your reality is conditioned to your perception of it. It was the American author Anais Nin who said, "*We don't see things as they are, we see them as we are.*" What she was referring to can be illustrated via the following simplified example. If you were to ask a pair of twins raised within the same familial environment what their view of marriage is, they would yield two different answers given their experience and past. Yet both twins were privy to the same nurturing, having been raised in the same household – so how could that be? Your view of reality is influenced by your internal landscape, since each person presents with a unique historical outlook, which colours their perception of life.

As you change your filter, this corresponds to a change in your perception of reality – how is this possible you might ask? Through inner transformation in the form of personal growth and self-awareness, your preconceived ideas of how life should unfold are distilled into your life's experiences. As you appreciate that life is more than what you know it to be, this will correspond to new and enriching experiences which show up in your life. We said it before – your outer world begins to reflect your inner most thoughts. Therefore, remain open to new possibilities by suspending your need to label or judge what you experience.

There are many people who do not even know they have these filters and yet continually react to their outside world. They believe reality is fixed. Your reality is anything but fixed. It is dynamic and pliable and mostly dependant on your inner world. Those who have achieved enlightenment have done so by transcending the material world – they are no longer limited to their conditioned mind. Their life view can be seen through universal consciousness – ever expansive, unlimited and non-linear. You do not need to be enlightened to experience similar states of being. You need only drop what you believe is true in order to make way for the *absolute truth*.

So how do you reveal your inner wisdom?

Well for starters, you have the same DNA as all the geniuses that have lived before you. It lays dormant waiting for you to access it. Here's the catch – it will not express itself unless you create a conducive environment for it to thrive in. You must be willing to provide the ideal circumstances for it to flourish by moving into alignment with the same energy as that source to benefit from the wisdom. Likewise, let go of your past conditioning by surrendering the false self. Let go of ideas, beliefs and thoughts which stifle your personal growth. Let go of what you think you should be and view life with a new and open mind – lose your mind as it were.

Similarly, become passionately curious about the world – live in awe and suspense. Think like a child. Question everything, challenge all things. The late Steve Jobs expressed it poignantly when he said, "*...they push the human race forward, and while some may see them as the crazy ones, we see genius, because the ones who are crazy enough to think that they can change the world, are the ones who do.*" This is inner wisdom calling out to express itself through you. Let it expand – allow it space to thrive and feed it with passion, enthusiasm and energy. Say YES to life – allow the energy of life to permeate through you. Become the expression of universal intelligence coursing through your mind body and spirit.

Wisdom is available to us all. It is the deepest part of our nature, much like the DNA encoded into a tree. We should strive to get out of our head and into our heart by connecting with the inner wisdom of our soul. The heart is the seat of the soul where wisdom resides. It holds the key to universal knowledge and intelligence. One must become quiet so as to hear the call of the heart. In doing so you turn down the volume on the incessant internal chatter that marks one's mental landscape. Create time to be alone with yourself in order to harmonise with your inner nature. As you become accustomed and attuned to your desires, your urges and your passions, your inner wisdom will beckon you to connect with it at a deeper level.

Cultivate Open-Mindedhness

In many ways unlocking your inner wisdom is a call to connect with the deepest knowledge which resides within, and yet it is simply more than understanding your thoughts or knowing your emotional constitution. Revealing your inner wisdom beckons you to connect with your heart and mind while your mind is the purveyor of universal intelligence. As you access your inner wisdom, cultivating open-mindedness becomes an extension of your inner state of being. To reveal your inner wisdom, you must be willing to cultivate a state of open-mindedness, rather than remain ill-informed.

Dogma and rigid thinking lead to intolerance, which in many ways describes the state of the world as it exists. Religious dogma imposes laws and principles which people must abide by to be deemed religious. Regrettably, if one strays from these principles, religious leaders and followers are quick to chastise them for going against their teachings. Sexual orientation is yet another case of fixed thinking, which gives rise to prejudices, fears and insecurities about other's lifestyle choices.

It is safe to say that close-mindedness stifles one's personal growth. I have met numerous people over the years who quite happily exist within their self-contained shells, refusing to maintain an open mind. In a world full of endless possibilities and infinite potential, I believe open-mindedness is the key to an ever-expanding consciousness. The following quote by the Buddha echoes this sentiment of openness, *"Let yourself be open and life will be easier. A spoon of salt in a glass of water makes the water undrinkable. A spoon of salt in a lake is almost unnoticed."* Whilst I recognise it is not always easy to be open-minded, especially when our beliefs oppose those of others, we can strive to be tolerant irrespective of our beliefs. We acquire our beliefs as we mature into adulthood where we begin to associate with like-minded people. As we are presented with a different viewpoint than ours, it can be difficult to accept or at the very least, be open to considering it.

You can gain a lot by opening the door to your mind, least of which includes having fewer prejudices, which fosters harmonious relationships. Those who are open-minded are more optimistic and make the most of life, since they carry less stress through their openness to change. Conversely, I have consulted with a number of people over the years who were fixed in their thoughts and beliefs. Over time and with the willingness to change, they naturally let go of their fixed thinking in place of becoming more open-minded. For many of them, it was an ideal time to surrender their firmly held beliefs and principles, given that many of these principles were formed long ago and had now constituted their personality. In doing so, they learned to carry less stress and are filled with peace and contentment in their personal and professional lives.

Being close-minded may impose on your personal growth and its associated benefits. Many people are resistant to change, preferring to remain within their comfort zone. Those with a fixed mindset dislike change, since they fear the unknown, of what change might involve. There is beauty and goodness contained in the world, that we must be willing to step out of our preconceived notions of what is right and wrong in order to experience it. Become like a child by marvelling at the world in awe – consider life through the lens of unlimited potential, conspiring to create a compelling version of life.

Expanding your mind by being open-minded, offers you a gateway to new ideas and beliefs. Although it is easier to remain safe inside secure boxes, venturing outside provides you with wide eyes to see the beauty and creative wonders of the world through spirit. Do you wish to travel through life being rigid and close-minded or do you desire to experience the richness of life by allowing your mind to expand? See new things? Try new roads? By surrendering control and letting go of firmly held beliefs, you make room for new ideas which are integrated into your experience. As you surrender control, you experience a positive manner of losing control. Often, being in control serves you well by being in command of your life's circumstances, yet it should not impose upon you by producing additional stress. Release a little of your fixed beliefs a little at a time. You do not have to transform yourself overnight. Experience new thoughts and ideas through a renewed and excited open mind.

Similarly, I invite you to change your worldview by viewing humanity through the lens of connectedness. Why must we hold on to the same worldview our entire life? What purpose does it serve other than to keep your thoughts stuck and outdated? The world is constantly changing, owing to the rapidly advancing information age we are living in. As we evolve and gain new experiences, meet new people, learn new skills, our worldview naturally expands to accommodate new thoughts and beliefs. Whilst it is not necessary to change your beliefs, it is liberating to feel you can if you want, since in doing so a higher level of mental and emotional freedom is attained. Moreover, as you consider new possibilities, being open-minded may cause you to feel vulnerable, since you must come to terms with not knowing "everything." This may be a positive outcome of your new outlook, since change and uncertainty give rise to new possibilities. Far too many people believe they have acquired all there is to know about life. I find it refreshing and exciting to know that I do not know everything, and as a result, I constantly remain open to new possibilities.

Open mindedness allows you to gain more confidence, since an open mind is like a vessel in which to pour the wisdom and knowledge of life into. As you maintain an open mind, you experience more confidence through your willingness to assimilate new ideas and principles. People who are open-minded are willing to change their views when presented with new facts and evidence. Those who are not are resistant to change, find life less rewarding and less satisfying due to their fixed mental ideals. To the open-minded, you appreciate that opposing points of views are acceptable, since it is not essential that you always be right or have all the answers. Being open-minded is like choosing to live in a glass house as compared to one without windows. You witness different people approaching your glass house with varying beliefs whilst observing them freely, but still have the choice to invite them in. Conversely, if you live in a house with no windows, you are not concerned about having people approach your house, since you do not seek the company of those with opinions that oppose yours. It is my hope that you will consider being more open-minded as you harness the power of your inner wisdom to create a remarkable future.

Awaken Your Authentic Self

In many ways to arouse one's authentic self is a call to connect with the deeper wisdom which we have been discussing throughout this chapter. Reflect on the following questions for a moment. What does authenticity mean to you? How do you know if you are being authentic? What measure of authenticity confirms we have connected with this ideal? Let us take a step back before we delve into these questions by considering the following. How do you know when someone is inauthentic? Is it via their language? Their body language? The way they dress, speak or facial expression? With any luck, you may have some idea how to distinguish inauthenticity in others. Now consider this for a moment, what are other people's impression of you when they met you for the first time? In his book *Mindwise*, author Nicholas Epley states the following about our ability to differentiate what others think of us, *"Knowing others' minds requires asking and listening, not just reading and guessing."* He is of course inviting us to engage our other senses in order to ascertain more about the other person, rather than form an inaccurate picture in our mind.

To reveal our authentic nature, we seek to suspend judgement about how life should or should not exist.

There is a level of discipline required to attend to those aspects which we dislike in ourselves. It demands courage to face them through an inner conviction and self-compassion. Consider the following statement relating to how others may perceive you, *"If I am aware of my limiting qualities, perhaps other people are also aware of them?"* Awakening your authentic self is a call to reconnect with your purposeful nature – the light of your being, rather than the egoistic mind, which rules your mental landscape. Release the need to attain perfection, since it is merely a guise to protect you from attending to something deeper that requires transformation. Free yourself from needing to be right, by choosing happiness, abundance, joy and love instead. As we have stated throughout the book, suspend your limited perception of how life should unfold or that it owes you something. Life does not serve to fulfil your every whim. You are the universal expression of life - it is your obligation to repay life by connecting with and revealing your authenticity. Say "yes" to life. Affirm that what you want is what life also wants. The more you acknowledge yourself as playing a larger role within the infinite intelligence of the universe, the more life accepts your role within it. Your authentic self reveals itself as life seeks to co-operate with you. In time, all your so called problems give way to new found blessings, opportunities and synchronicities, owing to the renewed sense of meaning and purpose, which you bring to life.

Our authentic self emerges as we develop a relationship with our deeper self. This means letting go of the false identity relating to who we think we should be and instead allows the real-self to emerge. Similarly, the ego plays its part in constructing the false self by convincing you of your inauthenticity. It does this by bargaining in the form of reinforcing your unworthiness, via a detracted self-worth. Every time you buy into this false premise, you strengthen the ego, by granting it power over you. The ego is self-serving and self-fulfilling – it needs to be nourished in order for it to thrive, otherwise it loses its identity. Without an identity the ego cannot thrive, since it cannot sustain itself without a reinforced sense of self. Yet, if we contemplate the nature of the self, we see it is a mental construct of the mind in order to create our place in the world. Author Michael Gazzaniga states the following in his book, *Who's In Charge – Free Will and The Science of The Brain, about our sense of constructing an identity, "That you are so proud of is a story woven together by your interpreter module to account for as much of your behavior as it can incorporate, and it denies or rationalizes the rest."*

As you weaken the identity of the egoistic self, you reconnect with your authentic self through your willingness to embrace your spiritual nature. Your spiritual nature is the unbound and infinite essence of your soul. It is who you are and will always be when you cease to identify with the mental construct of the self, in place of your soulful nature. Stepping into the light of your authentic self emerges, as you drop the mental façade of the constructed self. Once you have let go of this image, you make room for the actual self to emerge, which is grounded in authenticity. Secondly, strive to integrate your soulful nature and characteristics into the personality by merging with them. Remember, that which you oppose, you strengthen. That which you integrate into your experience, merges into the wholeness of your being. Authenticity then is a move towards unity, wholeness and integration rather than separateness. We arouse our authentic nature when we integrate our shadow self into the wholeness of our being. If we go to war with aspects of ourselves which we deny, we give life to the ego as it strengthens its hold on us. As we connect with the wholeness of our being, appreciate that we maintain an egoistic self. Yet our default nature is spiritual, we unite to become entirely whole as distinct from the wounded or broken individual constantly seeking to be fixed.

CHAPTER 14

Create a Purposeful Vision for Success

Create a Personal Life Plan

"Dream lofty dreams, and as you dream, so shall you become. Your Vision is the promise of what you shall one day be. Your Ideal is the prophecy of what you shall at last unveil." — James Allen

Having reached this point of the book, observing the past in a new light and considering the future with renewed enthusiasm, let us shift our attention toward capitalising on the lessons gained. You should now firmly believe that your past need not discolour your future due to previous mistakes or regrets. I am drawn to the quote by Helen Keller who calls us to look forward with renewed excitement, since the seat of opportunity may be just around the corner, *"When one door of happiness closes, another opens; but often we look so long at the closed door that we do not see the one which has been opened for us."* I would like to devote the coming pages in this chapter to show you how to create a purposeful and compelling vision for your future. I believe purpose and vision are two crucial ingredients in carving out a destiny filled with passion and hope. Passion ignites the spark, which fuels the flame toward desire, whilst collaborating to propel you towards a successful future.

Nurturing a vision for success becomes an exploration of the deepest wisdom which resides within us all – accessing that wisdom by allowing it to serve you will become as your focal point. As you undertake a masterful plan for your future, you unearth something that lay dormant within you all along. Vision and purpose coexist within the same container, which lead to fulfilling your deepest desires. A vision is the extension of your soul's plan made manifest into reality. As you align this with purpose, a powerful process is brought into action. I remind you of the Patanjali quote highlighting the activation of purpose. I carry this with me, since it serves to remind me of the wisdom we all have access to, *"When you are inspired by some great purpose, some extraordinary project, all your thoughts break their bonds: your mind transcends limitations, your consciousness expands in every direction, and you find yourself in a new, great and wonderful world. Dormant forces, faculties and talents become alive, and you discover yourself to be a greater person by far than you ever dreamed yourself to be."* Consequently, your purpose is your kindred spirit moving through life alongside you to navigate your life's path. Whilst your vision is the path toward that which you seek.

These coming paragraphs will be important to you. Whilst we undertake this journey with many different roads to choose from, seldom do we consider the time to map our life path or create a life plan. Many of you may have never developed a life plan owing to the fact that it is a waste of time. Your life journey is just that; a journey, so work on yours. If you are not planning or navigating the road ahead, you are bound to lose your way. In fact, there are plenty of reasons we should map out a life plan.

Here are several:

A life plan:

- Awakens your consciousness to following a road that leads to 'somewhere. The life plan assures you of where you are headed.

- Gives you a **sense of purpose** and a vision infused with life, meaning, and value.

- Prompts you to create tangible goals and action steps that will allow you to fulfil those goals.

There are numerous people who have put their passion and dreams on the back burner, believing they cannot sustain a living pursuing it. Sadly, life seems to pass them by and sure enough, they reach a point of no return, called mid-life, locked into a career and relationship which does not serve them. Sound familiar? In fact, a quick internet search on successful men and women will provide you plenty of faith that you can achieve what you put your mind to. Seemingly, given the advent of each New Year, many people contemplate their life's purpose with bewilderment. What is it? Do I have one? Believe that you do have a purpose – assuredly, it can be found by stepping out of your comfort zone and trialling it. While I may be stating the obvious, sitting at home while wishing your purpose falls into your lap may be wishful thinking. You must **take a risk** by creating forward momentum towards discovering your purpose. Certainly, the first step is the most difficult, yet the most important. Reflect on the likes of Bill Gates,

Tony Hsieh (Zappos) and Jeff Bezos (Amazon) who certainly never started out as business heroes. They began with the desire to solve a problem that many people were experiencing and create a value driven product or service that was the best in their field. How did they begin? *With one step.*

The attention turns to you

Do you find yourself caught in stagnation? Do you have dreams, visions, or goals for your life? If so, are they infused with passion and zeal? Are you happy pursuing them or simply too burned out to turn them into reality? If you are not enjoying the journey, it is time to re-evaluate the process you are undertaking. You might have to make a number of crucial changes, not only to your outlook, but to establishing firm goals alongside a life planning process. Take to the waters and **test drive your purpose** to see if there is a calling. If you fail, at least you have the luxury to learn quickly from your failures and adjust your course.

Let me ask you this. Where do you think you will be in five, ten or twenty years' time? What do you want your life to look like? Who do you want to be in the future? Most people automatically think about where they want to live, what car they will have, or who they will be married to, which is certainly fine, although I want you to consider what you want your life to look like in every way; financially, socially, physically and spiritually. Personally, I like to categorise my life into yearly components and within that framework, break them down into quarters. I also create a five, ten and twenty year life plan by apportioning it back to quarterly periods. This keeps me on track and prompts me to actively work toward my short-term and long-term goals. Create a life plan then allows you to gain clarity on what is important and what you wish to achieve over the course of your life. For many people life happens **to** them, instead of **through** them. Life passes them by at the drop of a hat and soon enough their dreams, goals and aspirations have fallen by the wayside as we have eluded to earlier. **Be clear on your vision** – imagine it, envision it and focus on it daily so that you are clear on WHAT you wish to achieve. Do not worry about the HOW. They will be made known to you along the way.

Strategize your life plan by mapping out a course which leads you somewhere, rather than anywhere. **Create your destiny** by stepping into it with a bold and purposeful vision for the future. A life plan can be a personal strategy and a call to action of aspects of your life which you value. It is an invitation to move in the direction of your life's priorities. Far too many people sail through life drifting from one career, relationship or circumstances to another. They have not defined their purpose or vision and so life eventually decides the course of their destiny. They fall victim to being at the mercy of life's forces, pulling them in all directions yet without having a clear vision for the future. As mentioned, psychologists call it the pain pleasure principle, which is the instinctual seeking of pleasure or running away from pain in order to satisfy one's biological and psychological needs. That is, people are defined by those who seek the pleasure of enriched encounters or simultaneously runaway from painful circumstances. If you continue to encounter undesirable conditions, your predominant motive will be to run away from your problems, in contrast to seeking new and exciting opportunities, which enhance your personal evolution. Form a clear vision of that which you desire by creating a plan which draws you closer to the life you envision. Enhance it daily as you gain a renewed perspective on your purposeful future.

Commit to Your Goals

We have established at this point of the book that creating a purposeful vision for the future is about connecting with the deepest wisdom of your soul. To represent your soul's vision into reality, involves laying the foundations to support it. The difficult task people often face is remaining steadfast in the pursuit of their goals. Life is demanding at the best of times, yet that does not dissuade the adventurist within us wishing to bring their dreams to life. The capacity to manage one's finances, health, relationships, career and a host of other things may leave us bewildered and lost while pursuing our dreams. Is it any wonder we often neglect those things which are important to us?

Relationships often fall apart when you least expect it, your health gradually deteriorates over time or you notice a gradual decline in your finances. At this point you remain perplexed how this all came to pass without seeing the writing on the wall. Managing your affairs requires dedication and commitment. After all, you are only human – it is only natural that life's events get the better of you. I am drawn to the following passage by author Richard Carlson, which serves to remind us to keep our focus on the bigger picture; *"Don't sweat the small stuff, because in the end its only small stuff."*

How do you remain committed to your goals when life is opposing you? Firstly, I would encourage you to stay committed to your path for the primary reason that life will continuously test your resolve to see how much you desire your goal. I have produced numerous video blogs via my website, while noting the ease with which people give up on their dreams. In fact, it's become fashionable – as a rite of passage for some. I can recall numerous reasons why people choose to give up on their dreams. It typically follows a dialogue similar to; *"it wasn't meant to be," "it wasn't fun anymore,"* or *"life is all about having fun."* The point is that our minds create any mental state we impose upon it. Through the power of belief, you allow giving up to become possible and thus validate it by looking for evidence to substantiate it. Success therefore requires discipline, hard work, perseverance, tenacity, will, courage and faith. With that in mind, I offer you the following motivational wisdom for helping you remain committed to your goals – no matter what life throws at you.

Leave No Stone Unturned In Your Desire for Success

In an ancient Greek fable, the playwright Euripides conveys a story of an army general who buries a large treasure in his tent, following his defeat in battle. When the conquering general and his troops could not locate the treasure, they consulted the Oracle of Delphi who advised them to look under every stone. The conquering general returned to the site where the tent was situated, ordering his troops to search under every stone until the treasure was uncovered.

The tale by Euripides, used since the 1500's, depicts man's unbending desire to pursue every course of action to achieve his outcome. Consider the relevance of this story in your own life. Is there a goal or dream you are determined to achieve with a vehement desire?

Giving up is an easy way out since it abandons the need to concede failure and the ensuing emotions which arise from defeat. Yet character is formed in defeat, similar to the process where carbon dioxide when applied with intense heat and pressure, gives rise to form a diamond.

Leave no stone unturned in your pursuit to realise a particular goal or outcome. That is, adopt an unrelenting desire to pursue that which burns deep in your heart. Have you noticed, those who strike upon success have an unyielding tenacity not to lose sight of their vision?

Similar to a dog who refuses to let go of his bone until he has gnawed at it, reducing it to nothing more than bone fragments, you must strive to exhaust all avenues before retreating into defeat. Often, we believe every course of action is being undertaken, yet something is always lurking around the corner, waiting to command our attention.

People who seek a cure for disease or illness, may spend years searching for a solution to no avail. Yet, as they abandon hope, a likely solution is brought to light when they least expect it. Therefore, I urge you to stay vigilant, yet in a state of expectation without a projected outcome of how your goal will come to bear.

Consider your answer to this question – what is it you desire? We spend a great deal of time protesting what we don't want, to the detriment of our true desires. Your subconscious mind constantly scans your innermost thoughts and daydreams. It does so by filtering pertinent information to reveal patterns of thought, particular to your character. Therefore, given your commitment, giving up should be the last resort until all avenues have been exhausted.

Similarly, what you set out to achieve may not be realised in the form you intended. Many of the world's greatest inventions came to life because of an accident or mishap. Consider the inventions we take for granted nowadays such as: post-it notes, Penicillin, the microwave oven, Velcro and x-rays. Such inventions arose out of mere accident and countless errors.

It is no surprise that vigilance, tenacity and an unrelenting desire are paramount in your quest to succeed. This principle applies to most areas of life: improving personal finances, career, entrepreneurship and seeking a committed relationship – think in terms of infinite possibilities.

In their book, The Winner's Brain: 8 Strategies Great Minds Use to Achieve Success, authors Jeff Brown and Mark Fenske state, "A Winner's Brain is very good at tuning out distractions and choosing the best way to focus on a task (there are different types of focus the brain is capable of) in order to get the best outcome." The ability to tune out distractions becomes a focal point to realise your intended outcome. The winner's mind is goal orientated, given its laser focus to stay committed to the project until it has come to life.

Regrettably, most people adopt the suck it and see approach to goal attainment, eluding to the English expression of, "giving it a go" while being attentive to what eventuates in the process. Whilst merit is gained in adopting this approach, it is better suited towards smaller goals rather than risk gambling in the game of life. A more likely strategy calls for developing a compelling inner resolve to pursue the goal until the end – far too many people give up, just when the tide turns. Whilst you may not appreciate how close you were, in hindsight you might lament your missed opportunity. Again, the timely quote by the late author and motivational speaker Jim Rohn, which invites us to reflect upon the value of regret, "We must all suffer one of two things: the pain of discipline or the pain of regret or disappointment."

Leaving no stone unturned in your quest for success requires restrained patience and biding your time. In support, a steadfast vigilance to realise a successful outcome is similarly paramount. I suggest you alternate between these two states, given that patience and vigilance tend to oppose one another. Do not abandon hope when all seems lost, that is the time when the tide turns in your favour. Life is bound by unexpected change when you least expect it.

Pursue everything in your power to realise your goal, then turn it over to the universe to usher in the ideal outcome. It was in Dan Millman's book, *Way of the Peaceful Warrior*, where he reminds us of the following affirmation, *"I no longer presume to know how life should come or go; letting go in this way brings a sense of freedom. This doesn't mean I don't care or have no preferences. My actions naturally follow the call of my heart, my interests, my values. I make efforts in my personal and professional life in alignment with my goals. But once I've taken aim and loosed the arrows from the bow, I can only wait with interest to see where it will land."*

Assume the same inner conviction towards your vision of success. Sure enough, when you least expect it, success will greet you in the timeliest hour.

Success Is Not a Straight Line

Maintaining success is the product of inspired action arising from the deepest wisdom within. Consider your current position in relation to personal achievement? Is success an elusive dream which seems unattainable? Are you the embodiment of success? Needless to say there are a number of people who attract success like a magnet, while others would not realise success if it was sitting on their front door. People often compare their success to others, much to the detriment of undue stress in order to compete with those who have attained more. Yet each person undertakes their success journey and no two people will experience the same outcome. Here is a typical example highlighting the need to compare ourselves to others. John lives in a beautiful home with an expensive car, he holidays four times a year and has a beautiful wife and family. They lead a wonderful and enriching life, through their exemplar work in the community and through philanthropic pursuits, which John and his wife participate in. What many people fail to recognise in this example is the underlying attributes which make up John's life. It may seem easy to compare another man's riches better than yours, without appreciating hidden factors, such as how long it took for John to arrive at that level or the sacrifices undertaken.

Jim Rohn suggested we should strive for "excellence," and not success. In our aim to attain success, it becomes elusive, like seeking happiness. If your focus is toward excellence, success is imminent since it becomes a by-product of the work and action undertaken. Returning back to my earlier question where I asked you to reflect on how you define success. How will you know when you are successful?

There are many questions to consider, yet if we do not undertake self-examination at this early stage, it may be too late when success finds its way to your door.

On a personal level, my definition of success has changed immeasurably over the years. If I was asked to define success during my twenties, it was comprised of qualities that a young adult would aspire to, i.e. become rich and wealthy, work twenty days a year and to travel the world. Success nowadays embodies a great deal more, as illustrated by the following attributes, which I deem as the pinnacle of personal success.

1. Impact on humanity through my work - guiding others to make their dreams a reality.

2. Being healthy in mind, body and spirit.

3. Maintaining a strong spiritual connection to source.

4. Enjoy lasting and fulfilling relationships with family, friends and loved ones.

5. Being financially free to choose life i.e. travel, work and buy things I want.

6. Give back to humanity through charitable and/or volunteer work.

I am successful as I tend to these areas of my life, measured by my attentiveness to pursue my purpose and destiny. Waking up from sleep in the morning becomes a joyful state in anticipation of being inspired by the work you perform. You notice that you are at peace with yourself and your surroundings since there are many detours and paths to take along the way. The detours and dead ends are valuable lessons gained in order to become successful, since they shape and mould your experience.

Having discussed this topic in recent times with a client, I debated a hypothetical scenario as to what he believed was required to make a million dollars. Moreover, I asked what is the mind set required to simultaneously maintain one's health whilst making a million dollars - also an appealing concept to him. He agreed in order to make a million dollars, he would need to step out of his comfort zone and similarly challenge his internal beliefs and attitudes toward money, success and wealth. Where he currently stood in terms of those beliefs, remained off the mark – there was a disconnection in which he sought to close the gap. During our conversation we explored the idea of pursuing health as a comparative view. We observed how easy and effortless it was for a number of health professionals to maintain a healthy body and mind owing to their knowledge and discipline in the area. I affirmed that tending to my health was like breathing in oxygen from the environment – my body had become so acquainted to it, it had become second nature. I often lament to identify with those who struggle with their health and wellbeing. I suggested to my client that in order to make a million dollars, he would need to assume the same level of thinking which he maintained toward his health, thus applying it to making money.

We can assume that simply adopting the same beliefs from one area of life is sufficient to influence another? Not entirely. It is well known that your past experiences shape your beliefs and thoughts. My client was yet to achieve the same inner transformation and inner growth as those who had made a million dollars. There was a gap between his desire and the fulfilment of that desire, which needed to be narrowed. Therefore, **past experiences** and **inner growth** were two measurable qualities required for influencing success. In assuming this state, success becomes a journey, not a destination. Read that again. "Success is a journey, not a destination." It is the person whom you become which determines your level of success. Research demonstrates lottery winners are financially worse off five years after winning the lottery than prior to their windfall. Albeit, winning the lottery may not be a bad problem to have, yet one must possess the emotional wherewithal to manage their newly acquired resource. Numerous winners lack the **experience** to manage that level of wealth and consequently it slips out of their hands – easy come, easy go. They have not created an internal shift pertaining to wealth.

As a result, the key to success is not defined by the destination, rather it is the person whom you become. It is the endless failures, disappointments, highs and lows which form the person worthy of success. I experienced a moment of despair long ago where everything I built was threatened. I pondered why I was striving so hard but earning very little income, while my friends were succeeding in their careers. They were enjoying success, whilst I was barely making ends meet and sacrificing a great deal to pursue my chosen path. Yet, such moments are pivotal points in one's life, since they highlight our willingness to turn our dreams into reality. I have grown immensely during those moments, having realised the deeper desire to pursue my goal. I am willing to undertake whatever is necessary, even if that means reading more books than the next person, working late at night to finish a project or seeking out resources that will accelerate my success - I remain willing and committed to undertake those sacrifices.

What are you willing to accept to realise your goals or dream? If life continues to present you with obstacles, are you prepared to push through them to realise your dream? Your answer will demonstrate a lot about you are and what inner transformation is required to realise them.

CHAPTER 15

Conclusion

A Remarkable Future Beckons

"Forgiving does not erase the bitter past. A healed memory is not a deleted memory. Instead, forgiving what we cannot forget creates a new way to remember. We change the memory of our past into a hope for our future." — Lewis B. Smedes

Contained within every personal transformation account lies a narrative of healing past wounds. Whilst we cannot change the past, we have the power to choose how we remember it.

I opened the book with the Lewis B. Smedes' quote, which contains a vital clue for inviting peace to a troubled past, *"Instead, forgiving what we cannot forget creates a new way to remember."* There lies our challenge and opportunity for inner growth – the power to form new memories within the present moment. As we gaze toward a purposeful future, we become less attached to how it will arrive, since we trust in life's universal wisdom to flow through us. In doing so, everything reaches us at the right time, corresponding with our lessons to advance our personal evolution.

As Marcel Proust points out, *"We are healed of a suffering only by experiencing it in full."* Our willingness to experience the past in a new light is matched with our readiness to write a new script for the future. This becomes the turning point for inner transformation. To cling to the past does not serve you other than the emotional baggage, which conveys the remnants of pain and sorrow. If we seek to create a new tomorrow, we must relinquish yesterday's memories in place of new ones. Often the past communicates vital lessons, formed out of tragedy and despair. Comparable to undertaking a road trip on a single tank of fuel, our vehicle can take us so far, sooner than having to refill the tank for the road ahead.

Similarly, in our effort to reconstruct the past, we reframe and renew memories by experiencing them within a new setting. It does not serve you to overlook the pain of your past as it does to discard one's personal self. Our wounds need not define us, owing to the preserved image of a damaged self. Yet it may be conceivable to draw on our past suffering to paint a new canvas. In doing so we invite peace and forgiveness to a perceptual world, which we no longer inhabit.

I trust you realise that you are more than the sum of your experiences. Any event which passes need not haunt you unless you award it power over you. As we continue to reignite and preserve distant memories, we extinguish the aliveness of the present moment by applying the brakes on a wonderful future.

I opened the book by drawing on mindfulness to connect with your surroundings, via your willingness to be attentive to the now. Mindfulness serves to reconnect you to the present moment than stay imprisoned, replaying tired and painful memories, which no longer serve you. As you harness the power of mindfulness, you build a bridge toward a compelling future by no longer clinging to the past. Your primary role to create a remarkable future arises out of the present moment and is vested in gratitude. It was the German-born spiritual author and teacher, Eckhart Tolle who reminds us of this powerful intention, yet overlooked action, *"It is through gratitude for the present moment that the spiritual dimension of life opens up."*

Gratitude does not involve comparing our self to others. Each of us is called to their own life's journey, bound by lessons and experiences specific to their life path. Consider if every person raised their mental and emotional frequency to reflect one of gratitude. The collective consciousness of humanity would expand, thus ending poverty, homelessness, war and disease. Gratitude is the gateway to a prosperous future, arising from your now experience and devoid of suffering. It serves to connect us to the past, present and future, while inextricably linked, serve to tension the beads on a string which hold it together. Each bead, whilst independent of the other, remains tensioned and joined to comprise the whole necklace. This is evident in the diagram below, illustrating the interplay between the past, present and future. Similar to the necklace metaphor, your past need not discolour the present moment. As we are liberated from having to hold on to the past, we trust a promising future beckons us if our desire to renew the past is resolute.

Past (Pain + Sorrow) ⟶ **Present (Gratitude)** ⟶ Future
(Anticipation + Detachment)

Similarly, we surrender the need to cling to memories, since we are inspired to see them through the eyes of gratitude. This state of reverence is available to us in the present moment and through our attentiveness to it. The gratitude we awaken in our hearts compels us to create a future filled with promise since we have followed our deepest wisdom.

Dr Wayne Dyer stated, *the future is promised to no one* – we stay in a state of appreciation of the present moment, since that is all we have. From this state of mindfulness, we create the future through our humility, attentiveness and awareness. To anticipate the future, whilst remaining detached as to how life should unfold, forms your present moment experience, projected in time.

I invite you to stay purposeful in your vision to create a meaningful life. Do not despair when life goes astray as it may be inclined. There is a hidden mystery to life's unfolding events, which the rational mind cannot comprehend. Your measure for a successful passage through life is gauged by your senses and awarded through your intuition and emotions. These faculties support you to take inspired action, via your purposeful self.

Stay humble and attentive to your surroundings – become childlike in your outlook. Do not become invested in your external reality if it does not conform to your inner world. Life can change within the space of twenty four hours. Keep a powerful and unyielding vision toward that which you wish to realise. Hold it in your mind and heart – nurture it via your thoughts, beliefs and emotional intensity.

The power of the human will is unbending – it can bring into being any circumstance once your resolve is strong. It was the British politician Benjamin Disraeli who declared, *"Nothing can withstand the power of the human will if it is willing to stake its very existence to the extent of its purpose."*

It should be obvious to you that nothing should stand in your way of the coming attractions of your life. Keep a powerful intention by nurturing it with desire and will. Although life undergoes change, continue to empower your desires. Step into your future by remaining grounded in the present moment. Embark to create a life you wish to meet by accepting nothing less than approval for your chosen path.

Reconstructing the Past to Create a Remarkable Future is more than stepping into a dream. It is the opportunity to cultivate an enriching life fuelled with fulfilment and desire.

I wish you success, prosperity and happiness and trust you find your way towards living the life you always thought possible.

Until then, stay attentive. Be purposeful and passionate in your pursuit of the highest truth; the wisdom of your soul seeking passage through you.

TONY FAHKRY

Tony Fahkry

Tony is a leading health and self-empowerment expert with over ten years' experience at the highest level as a speaker, author and coach. His understanding and integration of mind and body concepts bridges the gap between health, self-empowerment and human behaviour.

Tony has developed a comprehensive self-empowerment program, *The Power to Navigate Life* which he has presented to corporate companies across Australia. The program teaches participants how to achieve continued mental, emotional and physical well-being using easy to follow principles. His first book, which bears the same name, is testimony to the principles espoused in the program. The book has achieved local and international attention, with Dr Eldon Taylor NY Times Best Selling author, contributing to the foreword.

Tony is a regular monthly contributor to Bupa's online magazine, *BeWell* and is a consistently published writer, producing articles for *UltraFit, Women's Health* and fitness magazines.

He has achieved the highest authorship of Platinum Author for *EzineArticles. com*, with over one two hundred articles and 10,500 views. He writes for several leading health and personal growth websites, including *Pick Your Brain, SelfGrowth.com & StartsAtSixty.com* and many more. In addition, Tony is the leading author for *ArticleBase.com* with over one hundred articles on personal growth, empowerment, inspiration, health & well-being, mind & body matters and self-awareness. He works with several of Australia's leading CEO's and corporate executives within a coaching capacity.

Website: www.tonyfahkry.com
Twitter: www.twitter.com/tonyfahkry
Facebook: www.facebook.com/tonyfahkry
LinkedIn: www.linkedin.com/in/tonyfahkry
YouTube: www.youtube.com/tfahkry
Goodreads: www.goodreads.com/author/show/8306194.Tony_Fahkry

Lightning Source UK Ltd.
Milton Keynes UK
UKHW01f0628180718
325892UK00011B/1104/P